T0290526

Purposeful Museum Programming Using Visitor Response Pedagogies

Purposeful Museum Programming Using Visitor Response Pedagogies

Ames Morton-Winter

ROWMAN & LITTLEFIELD
Lanham • Boulder • New York • London

Published by Rowman & Littlefield
An imprint of The Rowman & Littlefield Publishing Group, Inc.
4501 Forbes Boulevard, Suite 200, Lanham, Maryland 20706
www.rowman.com

86-90 Paul Street, London EC2A 4NE

British Library Cataloguing in Publication Information Available

Library of Congress Cataloging-in-Publication Data

Names: Morton-Winter, Ames, author.
Title: Purposeful museum programming using visitor response pedagogies /
    Ames Morton-Winter.
Description: Lanham : Rowman & Littlefield, [2024] | Includes
    bibliographical references and index. | Summary: "Purposeful Museum
    Programming Using Visitor Response Pedagogies offers museums of all
    sizes and genres practical, accessible, and inclusive programming
    ideas"— Provided by publisher.
Identifiers: LCCN 2023058812 (print) | LCCN 2023058813 (ebook) | ISBN
    9781538186732 (cloth) | ISBN 9781538186749 (paperback) | ISBN
    9781538186756 (ebook)
Subjects: LCSH: Museums—Activity programs. | Museums—Educational aspects.
    | Museum visitors—Evaluation.
Classification: LCC AM124.33 .M67 2024 (print) | LCC AM124.33 (ebook) |
    DDC 069/.1—dc23/eng/20240110
LC record available at https://lccn.loc.gov/2023058812
LC ebook record available at https://lccn.loc.gov/2023058813

∞™ The paper used in this publication meets the minimum requirements of American National Standard for Information Sciences—Permanence of Paper for Printed Library Materials, ANSI/NISO Z39.48-1992.

To my parents who shaped my identity as a teacher, my husband and children who ardently celebrate my accomplishments, and to educators everywhere who show up for our children each day with full hearts and novel ideas.

Contents

Preface

Mastery in the field of education is a moving target. There are masterful teachers, to be sure, but novel approaches, contemporary discoveries, diverse perspectives, and emerging needs require repeated content, approach, and delivery reinvention. Just when you think you are an expert, you learn something new. I arrived at my career in museum education from classroom teaching, with a deep curiosity about impact, accessibility, and approach. Whether in classrooms or museums, educators facilitate experiences, even if just for a moment, that become part of our students' consciousness and emotional memory. Avoiding the facilitation of a negative memory is the ultimate goal. If you are a really fortunate teacher, perhaps you are able to deliver some new knowledge that sticks with someone for a long time. But content delivery is by far the least important job of an educator, and any good teacher knows that nothing is learned unless crucial social and emotional pieces are in place.

Through my instructional experience and coursework in museum studies, I have amassed a wonderful collection of teaching strategies, gallery activities, and program ideas but have also been left feeling overwhelmed by the wide variation in educational practice and delivery in museum settings. As museum studies professor Eilean Hooper-Greenhill asserts, "Knowledge is understood as that which is known by people. Facts are interpreted, or made meaningful in different ways by different people" (Hooper-Greenhill 35). In museum education, the opportunity and challenge is clear—deliver a powerful or meaningful experience to the visitor in a usually one-time, brief interaction that highlights something in the museum collection. However, numerous questions emerge. Considering that knowledge transmission is not always an appropriate or achievable goal for museum educators, how does an educator create impactful, purpose-driven programming? Is it truly inclusive? And since I am pretty sure that most visitors will forget a lot of the knowledge-based content that I am delivering, with what skills or memories are the visitors leaving? And here's the BIG question—did my program or tour really make a difference at all? With many questions with no straightforward answers, I desired a deeper understanding of what museum activities are optimal and how they connect to best practices in museum education, overarching educational philosophies, and defined goals related to a museum's collection.

Purposeful Museum Programming Using Visitor Response Pedagogies is what emerged from researching answers to these questions. It aims to serve as a resource for museum educators looking for a text that succinctly synthesizes ideologies of thought leaders and novel approaches being used in museum programming. The text is for museum education and museum studies students interested in learning about contemporary, applicable pedagogical theory and its implementation, or for any museum professionals who just want a bunch of great ideas to use in their museums. It is also for museum leadership who seek to further define "education" in their museums—how it looks in their spaces and how it contributes to their relevancy as an institution and connects to other realms of the museum. Finally, this book is for teachers who are looking for ways to use their local community museums to strengthen experiential learning and find new avenues for social and emotional learning for their students.

Purposeful Museum Programming offers a lens to help museums develop purposeful and meaningful programming, as well as a myriad of ideas and approaches within that lens. It is one approach—not *the* approach—but I make the argument that this framework, grounded in social and emotional learning and related skills, offers a powerful opportunity for museums to focus their offerings and make significant contributions to community well-being. The featured pedagogical approaches are applicable in large and small museums, from art collections to natural history museums to botanical gardens, and from well-known, well-funded institutions to the small, local museum.

The introduction makes the case for museums to further define their role in education and what that means. Chapter 1, "Things Remembered and Felt," defines Visitor Response Pedagogies and Purpose-Driven Programming. Chapter 2, "The Power of Experiences," looks at the case for social-emotional learning and defines the transferable skills of Visitor Response Pedagogies. Chapter 3, "VRP Activities Toolkit A–Z ," is intended to be a reference, filled with ideas for museum programs. My hope is that this chapter is bookmarked and used continually as a resource. For some of the activities, I highlighted museums using the techniques in admirable ways. Chapter 4, "Evoking Exalted Attention," addresses the applicability of this approach to different kinds of museums. Chapters 5 and 6, "Together We Can Do Great Things" and "The Questions We Ask," propose ways to start implementing and maintaining Purpose-Driven Programming.

It is my hope that *Purposeful Museum Programming Using Visitor Response Pedagogies* will spark ideas and encourage conversations about how thoughtful educational programming can enhance museums, demonstrating their importance to communities beyond their collections. By considering the purpose of their programs—both in terms of content and social impact—museums can contribute to the greater conversations of humanity, inclusivity, and our own well-being.

Works Cited

Hooper-Greenfield, Eilean. *Museums and Education: Purpose, Pedagogy, Performance*. Routledge, 2007.

Introduction

The Glowing Heart of Things

Over the past two decades, museums have acknowledged that their relevancy depends on more than their collections. Museum scholar Stephen Weil recognized the need for reinvention when he called for museums to move from "being about something to being for somebody" (Weil 28). The "being for somebody" part of that revelatory statement is largely demonstrated in how museums draw in and welcome a wide range of visitors and connect them to their spaces. These connections may be reflected in featured artists and pieces, revised contextualization and labeling, or community events. Educational offerings, however, are a powerful source of connectivity, and it is important for museums to harness the potential of their collections and develop programming that is purposeful, deliberate, and not just for *some*body; instead, museum programming must strive to be for *every*body.

As Weil posits, the success of a museum will lie in how effectively museum educational offerings are delivered (29). Despite progress and reinvention in many realms of museums, there is a wide disparity in educational programming among museums. As a classroom teacher used to working within (sometimes restrictive) curricular frameworks, I struggled to find cohesive examples of museum programming grounded in collective ideologies, educational theory, or evaluative data. Guidelines do not reliably exist—they don't really need to. Please do not misunderstand this observation—museums are filled with some of the most informed, creative, and hard working educators out there, continually developing and implementing fantastic experiences for their visitors. Certainly some of the variation in programming results from the wide range and themes of museums' collections and exhibits. However, many museum educators arrive at the field from a background in art, archaeology, history, or science, not from a background in education. Common educational indicators that help define what is important to teach, how to teach it, and how to assess it are lacking. Interactions with students (the visitors) are usually brief. The content itself is complex and layered with context. Although museum educators are dedicated to cultural responsivity and inclusivity, many programs are still heavily focused on historical or cultural contextualization and predetermined lines of questioning. Consequently, that shapes the visitor experience according to a particular agenda or staff's expertise, and this ultimately marginalizes some visitors.

Museums recognize and employ participatory and interactive elements in exhibits, yet these elements are not always embraced in educational offerings. There are copious, popular teaching strategies making their way into many museums—Visual Thinking Strategies, for example—but these experiences often stand alone and are not part of an overall educational framework or plan. Many museums, even the most well-funded and educationally progressive, feel the pressure to "teach," using traditional paradigms that focus on feeding their visitors "knowledge" related to their collections and exhibits.

Museum education also requires redefining and reinvention. Museums often include a commitment to "educate," this verb appearing in most museum mission statements. "Educate," however, implies a wide range of activities and outcomes, and museums need to identify specifically what they mean when they consider educating the public as central to their function. Perhaps a museum sees itself as a source of scholarship for a particular genre of art or culture, or perhaps a museum views itself as a space for cultural events or community dialogue. Weil identified four criteria for a "good" museum: purposive, capable, effective, and efficient (Weil 60). Integral to a museum's identity and relevancy, Weil describes, "a good museum is one that operates with a clearly formulated purpose, describable in terms of the particular and positive outcomes that it hopes and expects to achieve" (62). Central to this criterion, he asserts, is museum programming, although that is the hardest to evaluate. Perhaps one of the reasons for that is the wide variation in museum programming from institution to institution, which can cause a lack of clarity in purposeful outcomes that Weil describes. Desired outcomes of museum educational offerings are difficult to identify, vary from institution to institution, and thereby are challenging to measure. Simply put, it is hard to evaluate what is not defined. Even traditional, didactic offerings are challenging to assess in terms of their impact or "success." Museum program evaluation relies largely on teacher feedback if the experience was for a school group, or on other surveys that measure enjoyment or self-assessment of "learning" or growth.

One way to define a museum's purpose is by identifying cohesive factors or descriptors that trickle from the top down and touch all aspects of a museum's operations—from mission to curation to visitor services to staffing, and ultimately to museum programming. Inclusion is an important and relevant example of such a factor. Museums should strive for more than the accessibility of programming and should also focus on inclusivity in a broader sense, making connections with the community at large and helping all visitors to be comfortable with the work they are seeing, as well as cultivating a space where all visitors feel welcome and inspired. The concept of "shared authority" is applicable to this version of inclusive museum programming, as it does not stop at participation but instead dictates collective voice (Frisch). The autonomy of museums to embrace these ideals and implement creative approaches should be celebrated, particularly given the rigidity of so many other realms of education; however, museums need to consider how their educational priorities and programming contribute to inclusivity and relevant learning while also highlighting their collections. Some museums embrace this notion—sometimes referred to as "edu-curation" (Villeneuve and Love 17)—and create design teams that include museum educators from the inception of an exhibition. Edu-curators collaborate with curators, exhibit designers, and collections professionals from the inception of an exhibition, expanding the role of the museum educator. This hybrid process rejects the notion of educators developing and implementing programming after the development of an exhibition; instead, it considers the notions of shared authority and visitor-centered curation from the beginning. These evolving approaches work in concert with responsive pedagogical programming.

These visitor-centered practices also demonstrate how museums support visitors' well-being and serve as a space for connectivity. In a society that is not highly connected, many people struggle to avoid isolation and loneliness. Students' lives are increasingly virtual, both academically and socially, and this lack of connectivity is evident in how they interact with others and feel about their place in the world. When classroom teaching, I found myself with less time to review literary devices in *The Pearl* and more time needed to address peer interactions, students' exhaustion, poor organization, and social or emotional issues. Providing time for class connection and check-ins related to student emotions was increasingly part of my job description. A 2023 report from the Centers for Disease Control (CDC) and the *Journal of the American Medical Association (JAMA)-Pediatrics* confirms this with studies focused on the increased pressure on teachers to recognize and address student mental health. The CDC asserts that "while the primary goal of schools is academic learning, they also play a critical role in shaping mental, physical, and social growth" (CDC 3). Among the CDC recommendations is to focus on "school connectedness," or increasing the sense that all students belong and are part of a caring community. The need for social connectivity and a sense of belonging is palpable and not unique to school-aged children.

Educational programming in museums has the capacity and autonomy to affect their visitors' emotional and cognitive growth in multiple ways. Meaningful, inclusive museum experiences are best achieved by largely abandoning traditional, information-centric tours and instead implementing open-ended visitor response activities that are grounded in foundational learning theories and universal social-emotional themes. Some museums seek to be the authorities of their particular fields and may want to maintain their didactic programming while also implementing more response-oriented experiences. Either way, museums need to evaluate the range of programs being offered.

To make sense of my research and in an effort to answer some of my questions and satisfy my need for a cohesive lens for museum programming, I developed *Purposeful Museum Programming Using Visitor Response Pedagogies.* This framework builds on the ideas of many thought leaders in general and museum education, synthesizing educational approaches and instructional methods that emphasize visitors' responses to collections and enhance the development of transferable skills related to social-emotional learning and intelligence. These opportunities allow visitors to learn about art and other kinds of objects, draw connections to the world around them, and hone skills such as critical thinking and empathy. Moreover, these teaching methods result in experiences that cultivate a sense of belonging and enhance personal growth.

Museums must meet this moment. As community institutions, museums hold immense potential in combating issues of isolation and inclusivity. As writer and artist Bridget Watson Payne asked, "How do we punch a hole in the barrier separating us from the glowing heart of things?" (Payne 15). Her answer was art, widely defined as all sorts of objects for contemplation. By implementing inclusive practices and shared authority, and by cultivating important skills that transfer to other realms of their visitors' lives, museums can serve as a valuable resource for breaking down barriers and connecting us to the glowing heart of things. Museums and their gifted educators will demonstrate how objects of the past are able to teach more than their makers ever imagined, contributing to stronger communities and proving their relevancy.

Works Cited

"CDC Shows Concerning Increases in Sadness and Exposure to Violence among Teen Girls and LBBQ+ Youth." *NCHHSTP Newsroom: Centers for Disease Control and Prevention*, 13 Feb.

2023. *CDC,* https://www.cdc.gov/nchhstp/newsroom/fact-sheets/healthy-youth/sadness
-and-violence-among-teen-girls-and-LGBQ-youth-factsheet.html#teen-girls. Accessed 14
Feb. 2023.

Frisch, Michael. *A Shared Authority: Essays on the Craft and Meaning of Oral and Public History.*
SUNY Press, 1990.

Payne, Bridget Watson. *How Art Can Make You Happy.* Chronicle Books, 2017.

Villeneuve, Pat, and Anne Rowson Love. "Edu-Curation and the Edu-Curator." *Visitor-Centered
Exhibitions and Edu-Curation in Art Museums,* edited by Pat Villeneuve and Anne Rowson Love.
Rowman & Littlefield, 2017.

Weil, Stephen E. *Making Museums Matter.* Smithsonian Books, 2002.

Chapter 1

Things Remembered and Felt

Visitor Response Pedagogies and Purposeful Programming

If museums want to demonstrate that they exist for everybody, then they need to be accessible. I volunteered recently at an outreach event for a large museum, and not one of the participants (aged five to fifteen) had ever heard of or stepped foot in the actual museum, which was only a ten-minute drive away. Museums continue to miss the mark on serving diverse populations, even though many offer free admittance days or work in cooperation with outreach groups and school systems. Despite these efforts, many people simply do not feel comfortable in museum settings or feel like there isn't anything for them there. One way to address this issue is to implement programming that puts everyone on a level playing field and celebrates diverse perspectives while exposing visitors to the power of objects to awaken emotion and connectivity.

What Are Visitor Response Pedagogies?

The term "Visitor Response Pedagogies" (VRPs) refers to educational practices that harness participants' reactions or responses to art or other kinds of artifacts to build transferable skills. In education, transferable skills are defined as skills that are utilized in many forms of learning, both academic and social-emotional. An example of an important transferable skill is empathy and empathetic listening. Visitor Response Pedagogies reflect the growing trend in museums to consider the visitor's experience as central to a museum's exhibitions. Visitor Response Pedagogies consider these responses and identify skills that are reinforced. The particular skills identified in VRPs are explored in depth in the next chapter.

Addressing the "Visitor" in Visitor Response Pedagogies

An important component of VRPs is the focus on the visitor as well as the notion of the visitor as a shared authority. As museum consultant Mark Walhimer explores his text *Designing Museum Experiences*, "Museums certainly remain keepers of the objects of culture, but the meaning of those objects is shifting to the visitor. Museums are beginning to recognize that meaning is subjective, and depends on the visitor's identity, social background, and environment" (4). The visitor and visitor's interpretation are central to the experience or program.

The visitor is also an important component of the framework as museums seek to expand and invite more diverse audiences to the museum table. The museum prioritizes its visitors of all ages, from newborns to centenarians. To create more meaningful and inclusive experiences, museums must revamp their programs to cater to a diverse range of visitor groups and identities. This is where overlap occurs with the realms of museum education and visitor experience, often "separate" departments in museum hierarchies. Identifying community demographics is crucial for educators looking to serve underserved populations and understand community needs. Effective tools for this purpose are valuable in creating visitor-centered museums.

Museums identify important demographic metrics shaping the museum of the future. Access to and participation in museum exhibits and programs are areas of needed growth. A study by the National Endowment for the Arts in 2019 reported that overall participation in museums is at a low rate, with only 23 percent of the U.S. population reporting that they attend an art exhibit every year. Of those individuals, only 17 percent were Black and 16 percent were Latinx (Olivares and Piatak 121). Alexandra Olivares, an audience research and evaluation specialist at the Mint Museum, and Jaclyn Piatak, an associate professor at the University of North Carolina in public administration, conclude from their research that "museums can focus on access and inclusion by placing value in unique experiences they offer such as educational programming" (Olivares and Piatak 131). The American Alliance of Museums studies differences in attendance for various racial and cultural groups, noting that museums continue to be intimidating and feel exclusionary for many (Farrell and Medvedeva). In 2017, the AAM predicted that by 2040, there will be significant demographic shifts, with a 56 percent increase in seniors over sixty-five and a shrinking population of children under eighteen years of age. It also anticipates the rise in "museum schools," which include schools run by museums, and the increased role of museums in general education ("AAM's Museums"). Explorations of the museum visitor usually lead back to the need for inclusive practices, particularly in the realm of museum programming,

Considering the "Response" in Visitor Response Pedagogies

Another defining characteristic of Visitor Response Pedagogies is the emphasis on visitors' reactions to or impressions induced by objects in collections. This focus in turn de-emphasizes contextualization of the object and the associated meanings, as well as other metrics or descriptors related to the object. These may include information about the time period, the origin of the piece, the maker or artist, or design elements associated with the object. All of that is stripped away, and the experience is centered on the visitor, the object, and the responses it conjures.

The exploration of responsive activities has become more popular with the work of museum educator Ray Williams. Personal Response Tours, developed by Williams, facilitate reflective exploration of collections and shape meaningful museum experiences for visitors. As the former director of education at the Harvard Art Museums, Williams spent years "exploring the potential of the art museum as an environment that supports reflection, invites personal connections, and builds community" as well as "therapeutic benefits from their encounters with works of art" (Williams 94). His explorations resulted in a teaching method that focuses on "personal highlights" (95) and is initiated by participants blindly choosing a prompt or a guiding question and spending time exploring museum galleries to find works that exemplify or connect in some way to it. For example, a guiding prompt may be "Find a work of art that sparks joy and reflect on why," or "Find a piece that scares you, and think about the reasons for your choice." As Williams writes, "Inviting museum visitors to share their thoughts and feelings, memories and associations, is both powerful and unexpected" (96). Personal Response Tours have grown in popularity among health workers because of their ability to "promote individual reflection, foster empathy, [and] increase appreciation for the psychosocial context of the patient experience" (Gaufberg and Williams 546). Arts and Health Personal Response Tours attest to the ability of the method to be replicated in most museum settings and with most ages or populations of visitors.

These types of tours serve as one example of an effective VRP activity, but for some groups they may be daunting or not achievable. I have participated in Personal Response Tours when visitors expressed discomfort with the prompt they received or with sharing with a group. There are ways to scaffold or modify these types of tours, as well as dozens of additional activities that offer visitors opportunities to share individual responses to works and may be better suited for a particular group. Chapter 3, "VRP Activities Toolkit A–Z," is filled with activities focused on visitors and their responses to collections.

Defining the "Pedagogy" in Visitor Response Pedagogies

Pedagogy is the method and practice of teaching. Simply put, pedagogies address how and why teachers teach in the ways that they do. Pushing the definition further, particular pedagogies, or individualized pedagogies, are shaped by educators' adoption of particular theoretical concepts and frameworks that influence or even dictate teaching activities and methods. Educators may subscribe to a specific pedagogy or adopt the ideas of multiple pedagogies while forming their own ideological lens for the practice of teaching. As part of the Visitor Response Pedagogical framework, the theoretical concepts of transformative education and constructivism serve as a foundation, with skills associated with social and emotional learning as well as related transferable skills such as empathy and inclusion. With this foundation, particular teaching strategies and activities are identified and described.

Museums are well suited to focus on transferable skills because they are not required by any regulatory entity to teach a particular curriculum or defined body of knowledge in the way that educational systems are. Learning is a flexible construct in museums, and museums generally define their own learning agendas. Sometimes museums define what they consider "successful" outcomes, but not always. They apply an interpretive lens to experiences based on their own ideas, perhaps in cooperation with curators or local educators. This type of pedagogical freedom is liberating but sometimes unfocused.

Museums can support learning and educational systems by honing in on important skills that visitors utilize in other areas of their lives. Dr. Emilie Sitzia, a professor of cultural education at the University of Maastricht, writes that "museums . . . are perceived as learning spaces where the knowledge produced is not reduced to the acquisition of information but also encompasses the development of diverse individual cognitive skills . . . knowledge production in art museums is about giving the public the ability to acquire skills to generate further knowledge" (74). She refers to this "emancipatory cultural education" as one that allows a kind of intellectual freedom, which is "an essential pre-requisite to then tackle issues of representation, visibility, and power distribution" (74). VRPs take advantage of these opportunities to develop different, important skills and ensure a level playing field for all students while building community through planned activities. This results in an inclusive, validating, safe experience.

Figure 1.1 outlines the components of the VRP framework. In this and subsequent chapters, we will break it down.

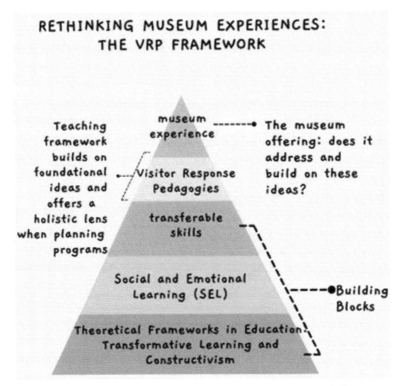

RETHINKING MUSEUM EXPERIENCES: THE VRP FRAMEWORK

Teaching framework builds on foundational ideas and offers a holistic lens when planning programs

museum experience — — — — — • The museum offering: does it address and build on these ideas?

Visitor Response Pedagogies

transferable skills

Social and Emotional Learning (SEL)

Theoretical Frameworks in Education: Transformative Learning and Constructivism

• Building Blocks

Figure 1.1. Rethinking Museum Experiences: The VRP Framework. *Source:* Ames Morton-Winter, M.A.ED., ALM.

Theories of Learning

Visitor Response Pedagogies are grounded in theories of learning. The concept or definition of "learning" is debated. Most consider learning to be the acquisition of new knowledge, but as Eilean Hooper-Greenfield describes in her text *Museums and Education*, learning "includes the acquisition of skills, the development of judgment, and the formation of attitudes and values" (34), and it "always involves the use of what is already known, and this prior knowledge is used to make sense of new knowledge and interpret new experiences" (35). In other words, learners cannot separate themselves from what is being learned, and it influences the meaning ascribed to whatever is being taught. This is significant for museum educators who are often tasked with transmitting, in a short interaction, knowledge that either they, their curators, or their leaders have decided is important.

Although numerous theoretical frameworks play a role in crafting meaningful museum experiences, many of the VRP approaches fall under the umbrella of transformative learning theory. Transformative learning was introduced by sociologist Jack Mezirow, who describes it as "the process of effecting change in a frame of reference" (Mezirow 5). Frames of reference are generally grouped into habits of mind or more established ways of thinking and points of view that are more malleable, influenced by the ideas of or feedback from others (Mezirow 6). When learning circumstances or activities are thoughtfully chosen, transformative learners move toward frames of reference that are "more inclusive, discriminating, self-reflective, and integrative of experience" (Mezirow 5). Art museum–based learning, through the lens of transformative learning theory, posits that students learn through experiencing something. This invokes "welcome feelings of introspection, reflection, and connection with others" and "promote[s] a growth mindset by encouraging learners to embrace intellectual curiosity, perseverance, and tolerance" (Chisolm et al. 736). As Mezirow further expresses in his writing, "An Overview on Transformative Learning," he identifies the need for problematic frames of reference to progress to ones that are "more inclusive, discriminating, open, reflective and emotionally able to change" (92). In educational practice, transformative learning aims to provide multiple perspectives on subject matter, such as giving students contrasting articles on a topic or asking a lot of open-ended questions that encourage students to look at a problem or theme from multiple points of view. Mezirow's ideas surrounding learning and students using their experiences to make personal meaning and sense of the world connect to another important educational framework, constructivism.

Constructivism refers to the idea that learners construct meaning for themselves, and it has its roots in the ideas of Jean Piaget, John Dewey, and Lev Vygotsky (Jia 197). These thought leaders posit that "constructing meaning is learning; there is no other kind" (Hein). The application of constructivist theory to teaching results in a focus on the learner's thinking, rather than on the subject or lesson, as well as the notion that knowledge is dependent on the meaning attributed to it by the experience of the learner. Education professor and researcher Qiong Jia at Shihezi University in China contends that learning is the "interaction between the subject and the object" and that "students enter classrooms with their rich previous experiences" (Jia 198), a critical concept when considering the interaction between visitors and museum collections. It is also an important consideration when designing museum encounters that validate and prioritize those experiences, allowing opportunities for students to share and express their thoughts when viewing objects. Moreover, as a teaching guide, constructivist theory focuses on the view that learning "is not the passive acceptance of knowledge . . . but instead involves the learner engaging with the world" (Hein 3). People can "learn to learn," and this often focuses on the language we use to frame experiences. Constructivist theory also claims that learning is a social act and is dependent on our connection with other human beings. In classrooms, constructivism is employed in group projects when collaboration is required, in a class debate, or during an independent research project answering questions posed by the students. Some of these strategies work in museum settings as well. Moreover, for museum educators, it is particularly important to structure the connection and provide an "entry point" (Hein 5) that is accessible to everyone. Constructivist theory has been recognized as important to the field of museum education since the 1980s (Yoo 375), but its translation into practice varies widely, from inquiry-based or "motivating" questions to facilitating sharing or reflection.

Both transformative learning theory and constructivism are foundational for new approaches to museum education—ones that allow students to consider their frames of reference and engage in meaning-making—while developing important social and emotional skills such as observation, listening, critical thinking, and empathy. Although these educational theories sound complicated, their translation to teaching methodology is not, and art and artifacts of all kinds serve as the perfect vehicles for activities that explore these transferable skills and offer an "entry point" for all visitors. For museums, both this entry point and the method of teaching are critical to truly be inclusive of all visitors. This is a rejection of traditional modes of education, explored by educational theorists like Paulo Freire. His "banking model" described learning as transactional, with teachers making "deposits" in the minds of passive learners. He viewed this as another form of unequal power distribution, with predetermined goals, taking into account none of the learners' predispositions or experiences (Freire). In contrast, transformative and constructivist frameworks in museums favor open-ended, interpretive learning environments. Considering the research of Dr. Emilie Sitzia again; she asserts, "The right learning environment can shift visitors' expectations of . . . museum visits from a traditional, guided, didactic experience asserting the authoritative voice of the institution, to an open intellectual relationship, allowing for discussion and interpretation and co-creation of knowledge" (Sitzia 81).

Many "close looking" techniques exemplify the idea of the co-creation of knowledge, directing students to look inward while engaging with pieces and considering how they feel about or connect to a work of art or an artifact. This allows the object to hold multiple meanings for different visitors and for visitors to determine what they learn from it. One of these teaching approaches is widely utilized—Visual Thinking Strategies (VTS). As creator Philip Yenawine learned as part of his research as director of education at the Museum of Modern Art, traditional approaches to museum education filled with ideas, facts, and skills "seem to engage audiences, but not enable them" (Yenawine 8). In other words, he found that students retained little of what was taught to them and that the museum's programs "didn't even empower them to be keen observers" (8). Creating experiences that allow students from all backgrounds to engage in close looking and to make personal connections are far more valuable than repeating the information on a label about the year a piece was created or details about the medium. As he explains, "Lots of what we see in art is common to daily experience. Art images depict people, places, things, expressions, interactions, moods . . . virtually all that we experience or imagine finds its way into the art of various types and cultures. An important aspect of art is that feelings are embedded in it along with information, triggering a full range of responses from those who look at it thoughtfully" (Yenawine 9). These thought leaders in the field support the premise that curators and educators must consider the inevitable insertion of themselves and their biases when planning exhibits and programs. Removing themselves from the equation allows for the focus to be on personal connection and learning through art rather than about art (Rice and Yenawine 299).

Despite this, a lot of educational programming still reflects traditional, didactic models, teaching art and design fundamentals—such as form, color, and perspective—as central to an arts curriculum, or historical and scientific contexts and content in other genres of museums. Many art museums continue to provide school tours that lead students from work of art to work of art, sharing titles and artists' names, artistic techniques, or perhaps stories and backgrounds related to the piece. Efforts to widen interpretations also stifle personal responses and connections to pieces. In fact, museum educator and former director of museum leadership at Drexel University, Danielle Rice, asserts that because of advances in technology and efforts to present multiple viewpoints, museum exhibits are overly interpreted—video, interactive kiosks, audio, and other contextualized information are commonplace. In addition, programming contributes even more to the interpretation of the exhibit or objects, adding to the noise (Rice and Yenawine 291). Yenawine calls this the "information surround" (Rice and Yenawine 293), and Rice warns that receiving or being exposed to a lot of new information does not guarantee that meaning-making occurs and instead runs the risk of directing visitors how to feel or what to think. Concerning museum education and the quest to foster lifelong art enthusiasts, future artists, and museumgoers, highlighted information or content is less crucial. Additionally, Yenawine and Rice's contemplations focus primarily on paintings and other forms of artwork and their own experiences at large art institutions. But what about programming at other types of museums? In the context of historic homes, children's museums, history museums, botanical gardens, and folk or novelty museums, the same principles and ideologies apply, and there are non-art museums experimenting with alternative programming. Some examples of these are provided in chapter 4, when we examine how Visitor Response Pedagogies may be utilized in a spectrum of museums.

Museums Are Not Neutral—But Can Museum Programs Achieve Neutrality?

Yenawine's discussion of the "information surround" generates important questions related to layers of meaning that museums purposefully or inadvertently attach to their collections. Dialogue related to embedded meanings of material culture is central to the question of a museum's purpose and relevancy.

Museum scholar Samuel Alberti's exploration of the "object biography," or agency of the object either realistically or metaphorically, ties into the ideas of the information surround (Alberti 559). As museum educators, we try to communicate the object's biography to our visitors; however, Alberti argues that we should not "attribute too much power to the things themselves. To do so would be to diminish the agency of the humans of the story . . . objects prompted, changed and acted as a medium . . . throughout their lives, museum objects were attributed varied meanings and values: collectors, curators, and audiences encountered objects in very different ways" (Alberti 561). The notion that an object's importance or meaning is dependent on time, place, and other external factors allows it to represent many different things to different people. In this way, Alberti's interpretation supports a move away from traditional didactics and toward response-centered pedagogies. In fact, he writes that visitors' "responses (and their traces) are symptoms of the relationship between thing and observer. This relationship is historically and culturally contingent, but it is never one way. However didactic and interpreted an exhibit, responses were a combination of that which was elicited by the display and that which came from within the visitor—things remembered and felt" (569).

Things remembered and felt. Framing the visitor experience in this way, museum educators must assess their roles in shaping what museum visitors will reflect on long after they leave the museum, and what they will feel either about the objects or, more importantly, about themselves. It circles back to the ideas of teachers as memory makers and theoretical concepts of meaning-making. As museum educators, our role is not to dictate the meaning or importance of objects. Instead, we aim to assist visitors in exploring their own responses to objects and acknowledge their relevance as perceived by them. In addition, we remain receptive to the perspectives of others with whom visitors interact during their museum visit.

An important conversation related to interpreted meanings and museum relevancy was initiated by the Museums Are Not Neutral campaign in 2016 by art worker La Tanya S. Autry and museum educator and consultant Mike Murawski ("Museums Are Not . . ."). They brought attention to the conversation about meanings that are attached to museum collections and perpetuated through curation and programming. Collections unintentionally convey meaning through their selection, arrangement, labeling, and presentation. Autry and Murawski garnered attention to issues related to questions of social justice and equitable practices in museums, calling for marginalized voices to become key to the conversation and draw attention to the swaths of people who are often rendered invisible in museums. This includes recognizing that what one "learns" at a museum may be different for each individual based on their diverse perspectives. I am not sure if the collection and curation of objects can ever be neutral; however, we might get close to achieving neutrality in museum programming. Visitor Response Pedagogies strip away "the biography" of the object, move the educator to the background, and make space for visitors' diverse interpretations and impressions.

In 2019, the International Council of Museums (ICOM) proposed a new definition of "museum." It was largely unpopular, and because of the COVID-19 pandemic, its adoption was tabled for almost three years. The proposed definition read:

> Museums are democratizing, inclusive, polyphonic spaces for critical dialogue about the pasts and futures. Acknowledging and addressing the conflicts and challenges of the present, they hold artifacts and specimens in trust for society, safeguard diverse memories for future generations and guarantee equal rights and equal access to heritage for all people. Museums are not for profit. They are participatory and transparent, and work in active partnerships with and for diverse communities to collect, preserve, research, interpret, exhibit, and enhance understandings of the world, aiming to contribute to human dignity and social justice, global equality, and planetary wellbeing. (Adams)

Although divergent from the long-held, rather short, conservative definition adopted previously, this reimagining of the museum expanded and enhanced the role of the visitor in defining their experience. Describing museums as "democratizing," "inclusive," and "polyphonic" put the focus on those visiting the museum. It defined the visitors' experience as dialogic and "participatory," working in "partnerships" with diverse communities to "interpret, exhibit, and enhance understandings of the world." The term "education" was removed entirely from the definition, maybe to distance the museum from connotative associations with traditional education practice. The proposed 2019 definition of a museum, while perhaps long-winded and pie in the sky, aligned well with Visitor Response Pedagogies and visitor-centric programming.

However, in August 2022, ICOM approved a new museum definition and reverted to a more traditional interpretation of a museum. The current definition reads:

> A museum is a not-for-profit, permanent institution in the service of society that researches, collects, conserves, interprets, and exhibits tangible and intangible heritage. Open to the public, accessible and inclusive, museums foster diversity and sustainability. They operate and communicate ethically, professionally, and with the participation of communities, offering varied experiences for education, enjoyment, reflection, and knowledge sharing. ("ICOM")

I appreciate the focus on service, community, diversity, and inclusion, but the rest of the language sustains the more traditional roles of the museum as interpretative and knowledge-sharing. This definition puts the emphasis back on those who run the museum rather than on the visitor and what they bring to the museum—their interpretations and relevancy in their lives. Regardless of how museums are defined, however, the ideals expressed in their reimagining are achievable through purposeful programming.

Purposeful Programming

Most museums agree on the premise that educating visitors is part of their mission, but arriving at a shared meaning of what is educative is harder to achieve. As George Hein explores in his text, *Learning in the Museum,*

> Our educational practices in museums follow some pattern, adhere to some theory, and reflect the beliefs of the staff and larger culture in which they are embedded

. . . we can make the effort to think through the underlying principles on which we base educational activities and shape the general educational stance of the museum according to these principles, or we can follow an unexamined collection of policies and practices that, taken together, present to visitors an educational position which may or may not conform to our desires. (15)

With museum experiences at the heart of a museum's purpose, it is crucial to define what learning looks like in that museum and how museum experiences will reflect it.

Explorations of visitor demographics and needs, responsive and inclusive museum experiences, and educational frameworks that allow for meaning-making and transformative experiences result in programming that is driven by a sense of purpose. This purpose or goal is not defined by specific learning outcomes or by particular bodies of knowledge. Instead, purpose-based programming is defined by several characteristics:

1. The program is inclusive. In other words, diverse perspectives and backgrounds (social, cultural, educational) enhance the experience and make it better because it pushes the visitor to utilize (and thereby strengthen) the skills emphasized in Visitor Response Pedagogies.

2. The program ties into defined goals that are not content-oriented but rather aim to support personal meaning-making and/or transform the participant by encouraging personal connections or responses to objects.

3. The visitor shares in the authority of the object.

4. Social and emotional learning is emphasized through identifiable transferable skills such as empathy (the Seven Transferable Skills of VRPs are explored in the next chapter).

When considering a new museum program or experience, museum educators should ask themselves if they are meeting these criteria. With deliberate, thoughtful planning and choices, museums will move toward neutrality and enhance their relevancy by implementing purpose-driven programming sharing these characteristics, helping museums create more cohesion between their offerings.

Works Cited

"AAM's Museums and America 2017 and 2040." *American Alliance of Museums*. 31 Oct. 2017. https://www.aam-us.org/wp-content/uploads/2018/04/museum2040.pdf. Accessed 30 May 2023.

Adams, Geraldine. "ICOM Unveils New Museum Definition." *Museums Association*. 31 July 2019. https://www.museumsassociation.org/museums-journal/news/2019/07/31072019-icom-reveals-updated-museum-definition/#. Accessed 30 May 2023.

Alberti, Samuel J. M. M. "Objects and the Museum." *Isis*, vol. 96, no. 4, 2005, pp. 559–71. *JSTOR*, https://doi.org/10.1086/498593. Accessed 30 May 2023.

Autry, La Tanya S., and Mike Murawski. "Museums Are Not Neutral: We Are Stronger Together." *Panorama: Journal of the Association of Historians of American Art* 5, no. 2, Fall 2019. https://doi.org/10.24926/24716839.2277.

"CDC Shows Concerning Increases in Sadness and Exposure to Violence among Teen Girls and LBBQ+ Youth." *NCHHSTP Newsroom: Centers for Disease Control and Prevention*, 13 Feb. 2023. *CDC*, https://www.cdc.gov/nchhstp/newsroom/fact-sheets/healthy-youth/sadness-and-violence-among-teen-girls-and-LGBQ-youth-factsheet.html#teen-girls. Accessed 14 Feb. 2023.

Chisolm, Margaret, et al. "Transformative Learning in the Art Museum: A Methods Review." *Family Medicine*, vol. 52, no. 10, Nov.–Dec. 2020, pp. 736–40. *STFM Journals*, https://journals.stfm.org/familymedicine/2020/november-december/kelly-hedrick-2020-0242/. Accessed 11 Jan. 2023.

Farrell, Betty, and Maria Medvedeva. "Demographic Transformation and the Future of Museums." *American Association of Museums*. Washington, DC, 2010. https://www.aam-us.org/wp-content/uploads/2017/12/Demographic-Change-and-the-Future-of-Museums.pdf. Accessed 30 May 2023.

Freire, Paulo. *Pedagogy of the Oppressed*. New York: Continuum, 2000.

Frisch, Michael. *A Shared Authority: Essays on the Craft and Meaning of Oral and Public History*. SUNY Press, 1990.

Gaufberg, Elizabeth, and Ray Williams. "Reflection in a Museum Setting: The Personal Reponses Tour." *Journal of Graduate Medical Education*, Dec. 2011, pp. 546–48. *National Library of Medicine*, https://www.ncbi.nlm.nih.gov/pmc/articles/PMC3244323/. Accessed 20 Jan. 2023.

Hein, George E. "Constructivist Learning Theory: The Museum and the Needs of People." *International Committee of Museum Educators Conference, Jerusalem, Israel*, Oct. 1991. *Exploratorium*, https://www.exploratorium.edu/education/ifi/constructivist-learning. Accessed 9 Feb. 2023.

———. *Learning in the Museum*. Routledge, 1998.

Hooper-Greenfield, Eilean. *Museums and Education: Purpose, Pedagogy, Performance*. Routledge, 2007.

"ICOM Approves a New Museum Definition." *International Council of Museums*. 24 Aug. 2022. https://icom.museum/en/news/icom-approves-a-new-museum-definition/. Accessed 30 May 2023.

Mezirow, Jack. "An Overview on Transformative Learning." *Contemporary Theories of Learning: Learning Theorists—In Their Own Words*, edited by Knud Illeris, Routledge, 2009, pp. 90–105.

———. "Transformative Learning: Theory to Practice." *New Directions for Adult and Continuing Education*, vol. 1997, no. 74, Summer 1997, pp. 5–12. *Wiley Online Library*, https://onlinelibrary.wiley.com/doi/10.1002/ace.7401. Accessed 22 Dec. 2022.

"Museums Are Not Neutral with Movement Co-founders La Tanya S. Autry and Mike Murawski." *Monument Lab*, episode 26, https://monumentlab.com/podcast/museums-are-not-neutral-with-movement-co-founders-la-tanya-s-autry-and-mike-murawski. Accessed 30 May 2023.

Olivares, Alexandra, and Jaclyn Piatak. "Exhibiting Inclusion: An Examination of Race, Ethnicity, and Museum Participation." *International Society for Third-Sector Research*, vol. 33, Jan. 2021, pp. 121–33. *Springer*, https://link.springer.com/content/pdf/10.1007/ s11266-021-00322-0.pdf. Accessed 17 Dec. 2022.

Payne, Bridget Watson. *How Art Can Make You Happy*. Chronicle Books, 2017.

Rice, Danielle, and Philip Yenawine. "A Conversation on Object-Centered Learning in Art Museums." *Curator*, vol. 45, no. 4, 2002, pp. 289–301. *Wiley Online Library*, https://onlinelibrary.wiley.com/doi/abs/10.1111/j.2151-6952.2002.tb00066.x. Accessed 17 Apr. 2023.

Sitzia, Emilie. "The Ignorant Art Museum: Beyond Meaning-Making." *International Journal of Lifelong Education*, vol. 37, no. 1, 2018, pp. 73–87. *Taylor & Francis Online*, https://www.tandfonline.com/doi/pdf/10.1080/02601370.2017.1373710. Accessed 19 Apr. 2023.

"The Twelve Transferable Skills." *UNICEF's Conceptual and Programmatic Framework: Education Section*, United Nations Children's Fund, 2022. *UNICEF*, https://www.unicef. org/ lac/media/ 31591/file/The%2012%20Transferable%20Skills.pdf. Accessed 10 Feb. 2023.

Villeneuve, Pat, and Anne Rowson Love. "Edu-Curation and the Edu-Curator." *Visitor-Centered Exhibitions and Edu-Curation in Art Museums*, edited by Pat Villeneuve and Anne Rowson Love, Rowman & Littlefield, 2017.

Viner, Russell, et al. "School Closures during Social Lockdown and Mental Health, Health Behaviors, and Well-Being among Children and Adolescents during the First COVID-19 Wave: A Systematic Review." *JAMA Pediatrics*, vol. 176, no. 4, 2022, pp. 400–409. *JAMA Network*, https://jamanetwork.com/journals/jamapediatrics/fullarticle/2788069. Accessed 22 Feb. 2023.

"VTS in Science Project." *The Wild Center*. https://www.wildcenter.org/our-work/history-of-vts-in-science/. Accessed 30 May 2023.

Walhimer, Mark. *Designing Museum Experiences*. Rowman & Littlefield, 2022.

Weil, Stephen E. *Making Museums Matter*. Smithsonian Books, 2002.

Williams, Ray. "Honoring the Personal Response: A Strategy for Serving the Public Hunger for Connection." *Journal of Museum Education*, vol. 35, no. 1, Spring 2010, pp. 93–102. *JSTOR*, https://www-jstor-org.ezp-prod1.hul.harvard.edu/stable/25701644. Accessed 8 Feb.

Yenawine, Philip. "Jump Starting Visual Literacy: Thoughts on Image Selection." *Visual Thinking Strategies*, 2003. *VTS*, https://vtshome.org/publications-philip-yenawine/. Accessed 23 Feb. 2023.

———. *Visual Thinking Strategies: Using Art to Deepen Learning across School Disciplines*. Harvard Education Press, 2013.

Yoo, Juyoung. "Bridging Art Viewing and Making: Constructivist Museum Tour and Workshop Programmes." *International Journal of Education through Art*, vol. 17, no. 3, 2021, pp. 373–88. *EBSCO*, https://web-p-ebscohost-com.ezpprod1.hul.harvard.edu/ehost/pdfviewer.

Chapter 2

The Power of Experiences

Social-Emotional Learning and the Seven Transferable Skills of Visitor Response Pedagogies

A person's experiences shape who they are. Being able to articulate those experiences and perspectives, label emotions, and walk a mile in someone else's shoes . . . these are learned skills with powerful applications to people's lives. More attention is needed to develop these skills, and the museum setting and museum collections can deliver these opportunities for learning.

What is Social-Emotional Learning?

Social-emotional learning (SEL) is the practice and acquisition of skills related to attributes or characteristics in the social, emotional, behavioral, and character realms of personal development. Personal responses and emotions are linked to the wider realm of social and emotional learning and the skills associated with growth in SEL. There is an abundance of support among educational scholars related to the importance of social and emotional growth for individuals. There are also numerous ways to identify and organize skills in the social-emotional realm.

One of the most well-known scholars in the field, Roger Weissberg, served as a distinguished emeritus professor of psychology at the University of Illinois in Chicago and chair of the Collaborative for Academic, Social, and Emotional Learning (CASEL). He argues that as classrooms (and society) become increasingly diverse in terms of social and economic backgrounds, students need more support in SEL to perform well, providing a safe, inclusive educational experience. He spent his career advocating for collaborative programs between schools, families, and community resources like museums so that "children, adolescents, and adults apply the knowledge, skills, and attitudes necessary to understand and manage emotions, set and achieve positive goals, feel and show empathy for others, establish and maintain positive relationships, and make responsible decisions" (Weissberg 65). Weissberg organizes social-emotional competencies into several interrelated domains that span cognitive, affective, and behavioral areas: self-awareness, social awareness, relationship skills, self-management, and responsible decision-making.

Social-emotional learning may also be defined by examining the work of the Wallace Foundation, a nonprofit that seeks to foster improvements in learning and enrichment for disadvantaged youth and the vitality of the arts for everyone. The foundation argues that "evidence points to the importance of social and emotional skills—including teamwork, persistence, goal-setting, and self-control—for success in schools and careers. These skills are developed over time and through repeated experiences in school, out-of-school settings, and at home" ("Our Work"). The Wallace Foundation model identifies three domains for SEL: cognitive regulation, emotional processes, and social/interpersonal skills. Their initiatives across the country in school and out-of-school settings aim to improve SEL practices and provide evidence of the benefits of SEL practices through research. A 2015 study by the University of Chicago, conducted in partnership with the Wallace Foundation, outlines a holistic, developmental framework for SEL, positing that developmental experiences happen in all settings and that "broader societal contexts, systems, and institutions shape youth development, often creating big disparities in opportunities and outcomes." The study identifies three key factors in the composition of a "successful" young adult, including agency, integrated identity, and competencies that fall in the social-emotional domain: self-regulation, knowledge, mindsets, and values (Nagaoka 2).

There are many ways to conceptualize SEL, but regardless of the differences in organizing and defining its components, the need for more attention and support is clear. Researchers in education consider social and emotional skills to be the "real core" of education and that "learning is a relationship and that the success of education depends almost entirely on the social and emotional dimensions of that relationship (Shriver and Buffet xv). Our world is smaller and more connected than ever in some ways, but arguably as a society we are disconnected and trying to make sense of its complexities. This requires attention and prioritization of social and emotional competencies.

The Role of Museums in Social-Emotional Learning

Museums are uniquely positioned to offer inclusive, community-based experiences and support social-emotional growth and learning. There are variations in how museums define learning or education. However museums choose to define education, it is important that they take the time to really consider their definition. Perhaps some will come to the conclusion, as the Mori Art Museum in Japan describes their educational programming, that visitors have "different interests, know-how and experiences" and that the museum's educational programming offers a chance to "share these while we come to understand" both each other and ourselves on a deeper level (Carlsson). Other museums define the role of programming similarly. Instructional designer and former director of gallery teaching at the Cleveland Museum of Art (CMA), Hajnal Eppley, argues that "in the aftermath of a global COVID-19 pandemic and racially motivated violence in the United States, museum educators must place intentional focus on clear connections between SEL and their museum collections to honor . . . lived experiences" (Eppley 509). She asserts that integrating SEL concepts into museum programming should be a priority. The CMA team conducted online programs that tackled three key areas of Weissberg's SEL domains—self-awareness, self-management, and social awareness—in an experience called Observe-Connect-Reflect that allowed students to engage in close looking at a piece of art, make connections to their lives, and reflect on how the connections might learn something about themselves (see chapter 3's VRP Activities Toolkit for more information). Even a simple activity such as this honors the personal response and creates community.

Moreover, offering opportunities that develop SEL contributes to equity by creating a common language or skill set among diverse groups of people with different cultural and educational backgrounds. There is growing interest in the connections between art and artifacts and this type of equity and personal growth. While at the College of William and Mary, educational consultants Dr. Gayle Roege and Dr. Kyung Hee Kim examined the interplay between student achievement and arts programming. They concluded that a strong educational framework "balances academic achievement with more holistic human development" and "provides opportunities for the interplay between expression and reflection" (Roege and Kim 126), particularly when independence and self-exploration are emphasized.

Museum experiences are particularly well suited to address the topics identified by these researchers. Art, for example, is an effective way for individuals to address and express their emotions, both through learning about artists and their motivations as well as through using art as an outlet to express themselves and connect with others. Researchers explore the importance of art and arts education to the social and emotional development of children and agree that "culture provides us all with ways to explore and create shared experiences, making sense of the world around us in the process" (Deakin). Museums, as art spaces, enable the exercise of self-expression, emotion, and imagination. They allow for exploration by offering opportunities to interpret the emotions of artists and connections to their visual representations of a wide spectrum of feelings and experiences. In fact, "art can help us identify emotions and consider how the outside world impacts those emotions" (Eppley). Because of this, "social prescribing," or medical referrals for museum visits and programs, is growing in popularity. In fact, in 2019 the Montreal Museum of Fine Arts became the first museum to hire a full-time art therapist.

Cynthia Robinson, the director of museum studies at Tufts University, explored the connection between museums and emotion as well, looking in particular at the work of philosopher and aesthetic educator Maxine Greene, who asserted in her text *Landscapes of Learning* that experiences in the arts help us understand ourselves and others more deeply. Robinson pushes this notion further, stating that the work of Greene and others unveils "the power of an encounter to help us self-actualize and connect, and the importance of an individual's perception to bring meaning to the encounter" (Robinson 148). She also calls for museums to address emotional connection in museums, writing, "We cannot push our feelings aside and expect to work effectively. We need to acknowledge them and help museum visitors do the same. Museums are rich with resources for this: now staff needs to get up to speed" (148). This includes museum educators and the programming they plan for their museums.

The idea of art and museum spaces as a vehicle for inclusion, belonging, and self-expression is increasingly accepted. Researchers and therapists Vicky Karkou and Judy Glasman examined the role of arts programming in education and concluded that "child-centric education highlighted self-expression, emotional development, and self-actualization as the main aims of the educational process," and that art education expands students' "emotional world[s]" (58). They also call for the implementation of new strategies and approaches to integrating arts education with other skill development. There is discussion among museum professionals on ways in which their institutions and facilities can be made more accessible and inclusive to diverse racial and ethnic groups. Partnering with schools and other outreach organizations to develop relevant and meaningful programming is a powerful way to increase accessibility and inclusion in museums. Research such as that conducted by Hester Parr, a professor of human geography at Glasgow University, examines these themes, asserting that arts and art spaces like museums "engender geographies of creative recovery, social connectedness, and cultural inclusivity" and offer "the possibility of being included in cultural and social life on equal terms" (Parr 162). Many educators view SEL as an equity issue and argue that these skills are "needed to navigate a complex social landscape" (Frey et al. 12) and that however you define or frame it, all learning is social and emotional at its core.

Museum programming, designed with these objectives, accepts and celebrates visitors' diverse ideas and identities, enriching and deepening the experience of everyone involved. Through art or other objects in a collection, museums are excellent incubators for social and emotional learning. Focused, purpose-based programming and educational experiences allow for a safe, inclusive space for community connections that help visitors examine their perspectives and the perspectives of others. This kind of thoughtful programming highlights the power of experiences to foster empathy, self-awareness, and other transferable skills along the way.

What Are Transferable Skills?

Teaching strategies that are considered part of the VRP family are grounded in transformative learning ideas related to people using their past experiences to understand new information, as well as constructivist ideas that negate passive learning and instead embrace the idea that learners construct their own knowledge and meanings. This type of learning is largely social and emotional and can be enhanced by ensuring that programming and activities are visitor centered and address one or more transferable skills.

Howard Gardner, most well-known for his theory on multiple intelligences, considers transferable skills as one's ability to apply a skill acquired in one context to a skill in another context or discipline (Gardner). Transferable skills are recognized as vital to a child's cognitive and emotional growth. The United Nations International Children's Emergency Fund (UNICEF) sponsors programs in various parts of the world that focus on the development of transferable skills, considering them important "to adapt to various life contexts and potentially transfer to various social, cultural, or work settings" ("The Twelve Transferable" 3). Museums are well suited to focus on skills such as these because although they are learning centered, they are not required to teach a particular body of knowledge in the way that educational systems are. Consequently, they have the freedom to teach what they like, embrace transformative and constructivist ideals of meaning-making and changing perspectives, and support educational systems in the process.

There is a broad spectrum of transferable skills. Depending on the context, these skills may include: identifying emotions and emotional regulation, impulse control, self-awareness, self-regulation, teamwork, relationship building, decision-making, organizational skills, conflict resolution, attention, sharing, empathy, leadership, self-confidence, self-efficacy, resiliency, creativity, perseverance and grip, growth mindset, coping, stress management, goal setting, communication skills, or even ethics.

Museum experiences are limited by many factors, but the biggest one is that most interactions between visitors and museum educators are fleeting. Some programs may be multipart, and some visitors may visit regularly as members, but generally speaking museum programs are thirty to sixty minutes from start to finish and are usually one-time interactions. So although organizational skills and conflict resolution are important transferable skills, the museum setting may not be the most appropriate for their reinforcement (although I am sure there are ways to do it!). I have identified seven skills that are applicable to most museums and programs and are realistic skills to reinforce within a limited time and setting.

There is one area that some SEL scholars identify as a transferable skill that I did not include—creativity. Creativity may seem like a natural match for a museum setting; however, it is generally thought of as a complex transferable skill, in that its utilization depends on the successful use of multiple other skills. For example, when using oral communication skills, being creative may help in presenting or expressing an idea. Creativity may be helpful when collaborating or problem-solving. I consider creativity as a natural part of any learning process. In museums, there are ample opportunities to look at something in creative ways or use creativity in museum programs such as art making; however, it is not addressed as a distinct teachable skill in relation to this framework or the activities presented. There are art-making extension activities proposed in chapter 3's VRP Activities Toolkit, all of which offer visitors additional chances to "create."

The Seven Transferable Skills of Visitor Response Pedagogies

VRPs recognize seven areas of learning that are vital in both social and cognitive development and that museums can reinforce in their programming. Not only does development of these skills enhance the connection to the museum experience and interaction with art and objects, but attention to these skills also impacts visitors long after they leave the museum and enter a school classroom, a workplace, or a host of other situations. This relates back to the questions museum educator Philip Yenawine asked regarding what "sticks" with visitors after they leave the museum. Other practitioners in the field ask similar questions about the types of educational practice that make the greatest impact. For example, Rochelle Wolberg, curator-director of Mounts Botanical Garden, and Allison Goff, visitor services director at Henry Morrison Flagler Museum (both in Palm Beach County, Florida) explored practices like thinking routines and assessed their effect in terms of educational gain. In their examination, they concluded that at the Flagler Museum, "one goal of the education department's school-based programming is to become an extension of the traditional classroom, to be a resource for teachers and students where learning continues and connections are made," and that unless thought is given to the types of approaches being implemented, "a museum tour or program is an esoteric experience outside of the classroom and often results in little or no transference beyond that isolated experience" (Wolberg and Goff 64). While there is value in simply spending a day at a museum, museums can do more to move the learning needle for visitors and ensure that they walk away with new skills.

The seven transferable skills identified by Visitor Response Pedagogies include: Active Listening, Close Looking/Observation, Collaboration, Communication, Critical Thinking, Empathy, and Self-Awareness. Let's examine each of these more deeply.

Active Listening

Active Listening asks learners to be attentive and responsive to others when they express themselves or provide input. It requires the listener to connect emotionally to others and even repeat or convey the other's expression after actively listening. Active Listening requires individuals to withhold judgment. The United States Institute of Peace describes this kind of listening as more of a way of responding, in that it ensures speakers that they have been heard. It includes non-verbal cues, such as eye contact, leaning forward or nodding, sitting still, and letting the speaker finish without interruption. It also includes verbal cues such as restating or paraphrasing what someone says, reflecting on what was said, and asking open-ended questions such as "How did you feel about that?" ("What Is Active Listening?"). When people actively listen, they are deeply engaged in what is being said.

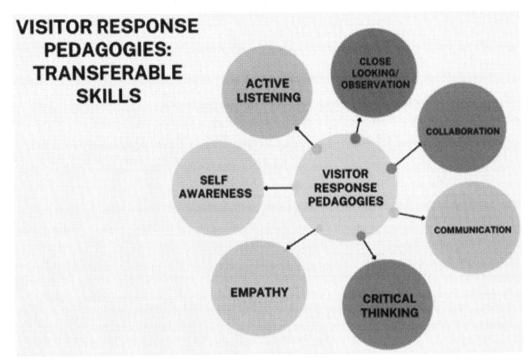

VISITOR RESPONSE PEDAGOGIES: TRANSFERABLE SKILLS

ACTIVE LISTENING

CLOSE LOOKING/ OBSERVATION

COLLABORATION

SELF AWARENESS

VISITOR RESPONSE PEDAGOGIES

COMMUNICATION

EMPATHY

CRITICAL THINKING

Figure 2.1. Visitor Response Pedagogies: Transferable Skills. *Source:* Ames Morton-Winter, M.A.ED., ALM.

When the listener does speak, it reflects the ability to step into another person's frame of reference (part of those transformative learning frameworks discussed in chapter 1). Some refer to the paraphrasing portion of Active Listening as "reframing." Reframing offers the opportunity for listeners to confirm what they heard by describing it in their own words. It allows listeners to visualize a situation or hear about someone's experience and shift their understanding of it. Speakers are validated when what they share is summarized and specific details are confirmed with them. One approach that depends heavily on Active Listening is Visual Thinking Strategies. VTS uses reframing in facilitated conversations. Following responses to the question, "What do you see in this picture?" the facilitator paraphrases the participants' observations (e.g., "You expressed that you feel the gaze of this figure on the right seems lonely as they stare, sort of expressionless, out the window"), offering opportunities to validate perspectives, elevate or introduce new vocabulary, and use inclusive language. Active Listening builds connection and helps people feel comfortable sharing, which in turn contributes to the development of other important transferable skills such as Empathy.

Close Looking/Observation

Close Looking (also referred to as Slow Looking) is the skill of examining something in great detail—an image, a piece of writing, a specimen, or a situation—and from many perspectives to gain information. It is foundational to Visitor Response Pedagogies and the development of transferable skills. Close Looking is a state of mind more than a measurement of one's ability to take note of many things in a piece. It is a mindset that encourages an individual to slow down and feel comfortable staying with a piece for several minutes. This practice usually results in seeing something—like a work of art—in new and diverse ways. Mastery of this skill results in an increased ability to act as a keen observer and connect more with art, objects, situations, or surroundings.

Shari Tishman, a senior researcher at Project Zero at Harvard University, is largely credited with bringing the slow-looking movement to the forefront of museum education by emphasizing that people learn a great deal by honing their observational skills. In her book *The Art and Practice of Learning through Observation*, Tishman makes a case for inquiry-based learning and provides strategies for looking to maximize the learning experience, claiming that detailed descriptions act as "cognitive frames" for thinking about art and objects. She states that "when it comes to slow looking, description primarily relates to phenomena that are observable through the senses" (49). Project Zero at Harvard University's Graduate School of Education examines Slow or Close Looking in myriad ways, analyzing it as an effective teaching strategy and even more so as a new way of life or a way of doing things. Their website is extensive, with countless applications of the practice and pedagogical connections, including a toolbox as part of its Creative Communities of Innovation initiative providing the "steps" of Close Looking, and an introduction to thinking practices, or "thinking routines" as they refer to them.

Other museum researchers and educators explore the importance of observation in transformational educational experiences. For example, Nicola Giardina developed a framework called the Pyramid of Inquiry while working at the Metropolitan Museum of Art. This focus of art inquiry is grounded in Close Looking or Observation. Her main focus is critical thinking skills, as she asks learners to engage in evidence-based inference that leads to interpretation; however, she also connects her method of inquiry to social and emotional development, linking it to engagement that inspires awe and wonder. She writes, "When we investigate works of art together, we learn to see through each other's eyes . . . you are building community within your class and teaching essential skills of empathy and understanding. Collaborative meaning-making depends on the strength in diversity." She also asserts that "students gain confidence in their ideas and their individual ways of seeing the world" (Giardina 3). As Observation is the first step in most VRP activities, an understanding of Close Looking practice and keen Observation is important.

Collaboration

Collaboration is an important prosocial skill, and it works in tandem with other transferable skills. Collaboration generally refers to people working together to achieve a common purpose. In museum programs, collaboration can be practiced by creating a task that can only be completed with everyone's participation, and it is important to structure the task or activity with that in mind. For example, simply telling partners or a group to work together may not be adequate. The activity must require input from each participant, such as Group Poetry in which each individual contributes two lines of poetry based on a piece of art or artifact (see chapter 3's VRPs Activities Toolkit). Collaborative activities focus on working with others by developing cooperative skills and expectations surrounding participation and negotiation. Collaboration requires cooperation, the ability to work well with diverse people, and the arrival at shared decisions with shared responsibilities. It also requires a display of trust in and respect for fellow collaborators and a belief that the contributions of others are valuable. Collaboration helps mitigate competitive tendencies, contributing to social cohesion and the collective good.

Communication

Communication is another skill area emphasized in many educational standards, and it stresses the ability to express one's thoughts or opinions and provide evidence or reasoning for those. Oral communication is a particularly useful transferable skill, but there are other valuable ways to communicate, such as writing or drawing, if oral skills are not accessible for certain individuals.

What is central to communication skills is the ability to exchange information in an effective and respectful way. One could make an argument that all other expressions of skills are dependent on the ability to communicate accurately and effectively. Certainly, Active Listening, Collaboration, and Critical Thinking are highly dependent on good communication.

Critical Thinking

Critical Thinking receives a great deal of attention in the field of education as it is a skill required in all academic realms. Critical Thinking requires an objective analysis or evaluation of a topic or subject from which a judgment or opinion is formed. It is the first step in problem-solving and leads to making decisions. It involves asking questions, identifying assumptions, and evaluating facts, and it is "a fundamental skill to understand a world in constant change" ("The Twelve Transferable"). In practice, this may result in learners that are able to separate facts from opinions, question the validity of something, and result in keen listening and observational skills. It plays a crucial role in most academic subjects in school and transfers into everyday life and work. Additionally, it is a skill that can be explicitly taught, and for those from diverse socioeconomic and/or cultural backgrounds, it may or may not be valued or given as much attention. Reflecting on our brief discussion of Freire's "banking model" of education, Critical Thinking rejects the student or visitor as an empty vessel being acted upon or filled with predetermined ideas and information. Instead, it promotes and encourages the questioning of facts and opinions and is an important skill that allows learners to determine the value and validity of information independently. In an increasingly digital world, this is crucial. In museums, educators can encourage Critical Thinking by using arts and other objects as subjects for questioning and evaluation.

Empathy

The importance of **Empathy** in pedagogical approach and practice is widely recognized. Empathy is the ability to understand the emotions of others. There are scholars that view Empathy as an emotion and some that view it as a skill, as I do in this discussion. Either as a skill or an emotion, we need more of it. As President Barack Obama stated in a town hall speech in 2008, "The biggest deficit we have in our society and in the world right now is an empathy deficit. We are in great need of people being able to stand in somebody else's shoes and see the world through their eyes." There are overlaps between Empathy and emotional intelligence or quotient (EQ), although they are often used interchangeably. EQ is broader in its definition, which includes the ability not only to understand emotions but also to manage or regulate emotions. Empathizing is often seen as a marker of advanced EQ, and many transferable skills are considered to be under the EQ umbrella.

The role of museums in fostering empathy is often debated. Elif M. Gokcigdem, the author of *Fostering Empathy through Museums*, argues that visitors may "gain a perspective-altering lens that awakens our sense of connectedness, respect, compassion, presence, and purpose" (Gokcigdem xxiii). She asserts that "through their social and educational mission, museums can provide a safe space for encountering our collective behavior, knowledge, complex histories, and values. By putting people in proximity to other people's lived experiences, the artifacts from their cultures, and their stories, museums can help us awaken to different realities and multiple perspectives that exist around us (Gokcigdem "Five Ways"). Certainly, art and artifacts of all kinds serve as vehicles to explore Empathy, compassion, and other emotions. Visitors can use art to identify feelings a subject may be expressing, examine artifacts to explore historical empathy, or study current challenges of artists around the world, such as those in war zones. There are some scholars, however, who criticize the use of museum collections to elicit emotional responses from its visitors, believing that "empathy can be offered—or withheld—and these are choices that are individual, social in nature, and often political and ideological" (Campbell and Smith 299). In other words, visitors should feel like they can exercise Empathy or not.

Labeling feelings is the first step in using Empathy in responsive activities, as well as guiding people to use affective statements or "I" statements ("I feel worried about the subject in this photo because they look like they might be in danger," for example). The goal of the exhibit or related programming should be emotional insight, not dictating a particular emotion with a predetermined narrative or expected response. Activities that explore Empathy should be designed to allow visitors to name and express the emotions they are feeling. Certainly, Visitor Response Pedagogies aim to be open-ended and accepting of visitors' individualized responses to collections.

That said, it is hard to ignore the power of art and objects to offer opportunities to develop collective empathy. A photograph of an emaciated polar bear in its melting habitat, or thousands of prisoners' shoes piled in a display in the United States Holocaust Memorial Museum, are going to conjure strong responses from visitors, but they may not be in alignment. Accepting the perspectives of others, even when they are oppositional, is part of being inclusive and is a result of Active Listening, as well as part of emotional regulation. Museum educators need to be prepared for a range of responses to most activities, particularly when they are not traditionally didactic; however, shying away from museum activities that explore emotional responses and help develop emotional vocabulary is a missed opportunity to nurture an important transferable skill.

Some institutions are embracing themes surrounding Empathy and diving in headfirst. For example, in April 2022 East Tennessee State University presented seven pop-up exhibits as part of an Empathy Museum. Each of the exhibits was designed to have visitors put themselves in someone else's shoes, with the goal of cultivating compassion and understanding for other people. For example, the exhibit "The Sound of Silence" challenged visitors to attempt to read lips while wearing noise-canceling headphones, while "Pay to Fail" included a simulation game that mimicked food scarcity by providing a limited budget and a shopping list for a large family. Another exhibit that receives attention is "The Lunch Counter" simulation at the Center for Civil and Human Rights in Atlanta, which asks visitors to sit on dining stools where a sign reads, "How long can you last?" Visitors, using headphones, experience being ignored, insulted, and even physically impacted with kicks and shoves to the stools. These types of experiential learning opportunities ask visitors to name their emotions and consider the perspectives of those who endured these interactions regularly. Experiences that encourage empathetic responses may also encourage emotions like surprise or amazement, such as offering a perspective on space exploration or introducing someone who overcame a challenge to produce something beautiful. As museum educators, we can look for opportunities to develop empathetic perspectives and allow visitors a safe space to name the emotions they experience while interacting with a museum's collection or exhibit.

Self-Awareness

Self-Awareness is the ability to look inward and reflect on one's emotions, values, and behaviors, as well as identify one's strengths and weaknesses. The Collaborative for Academic, Social, and Emotional Learning (CASEL) identifies it as a key competency in SEL. The ability to recognize the components of self-awareness helps to develop resiliency and flexibility in unexpected or changing circumstances. A long-range study involving nearly five thousand participants examined what

Self-Awareness is and what it is not, revealing that it is a highly valued transferable skill, but that it is also a relatively rare quality in individuals (Eurich). The research team identified two types of Self-Awareness: internal and external. Internal Self-Awareness represents how individuals see themselves (values, passions, etc.), and external Self-Awareness refers to how other people view them and how the outside world impacts or plays a role in that.

Inclusion also plays a role in developing Self-Awareness and is a skill in its own right. Inclusion refers not only to the practice of providing equal access to an opportunity but also to an awareness or sensitivity to the fact that all students are accessing the opportunity from diverse contexts or experiences. It falls under the umbrella of Self-Awareness because it requires individuals to hold a mirror to themselves and recognize their own biases and perspectives based on numerous factors—culture, race, socioeconomics, family makeup, health, or gender, just to name a few. For example, the use of inclusive language that avoids biases or discriminatory slang is part of this skill set.

These seven skills are by no means comprehensive, and I view the list as fluid; however, they serve as jumping-off points for connected, purpose-based programming.

Works Cited

Carlsson, Rebecca. "Are Museums Good for Your Mental Health?" *MuseumNext,* 4 Aug. 2022. *MuseumNext,* https://www.museumnext.com/article/are-museums-good-for-your-mental -health/. Accessed 19 June 2023.

Deakin, Tim. "The Role of Museums in Supporting the Wellbeing of Children and Families." *MuseumNext,* 11 Jan. 2022. *MuseumNext,* https://www.museumnext.com/article/the-role-of -museums-in-supporting-the-wellbeing-of-children-and-families/. Accessed 16 Dec. 2022.

Eppley, Hajnal. "How Art Supports Emotional Wellness." *Medium.com.* 30 Sept. 2020. *Medium,* https://clevelandmuseumofart.medium.com/how-art-supports-emotional-wellness -e3e1aff6afda. Accessed 12 Nov. 2020.

———. "Museums as Partners in PreK-12 Social-Emotional Learning." *Journal of Museum Education,* vol. 46, no. 4, 2021, pp. 509–18, https://doi.org/10.1080/10598650.2021.1979299.

Eurich, Tasha. "What Self-Awareness Really Is (and How to Cultivate It)." *Harvard Business Review,* 4 Jan. 2008. https://hbr.org/2018/01/what-self-awareness-really-is-and-how-to-cultivate -it. Accessed 29 June 2023.

Frey, Nancy, et al. *All Learning Is Social and Emotional: Helping Students Develop Essential Skills for the Classroom and Beyond.* ACSD, 2019.

Gardner, Howard. *The Disciplined Mind: What All Students Should Understand.* New York, Simon & Schuster, 1999.

Giardina, Nicola. *The More We Look, The Deeper We Get: Transforming the Curriculum through Art.* Rowman & Littlefield, 2018.

Gokcigdem, Elif M. "Five Ways Museums Can Increase Empathy in the World." *Greater Good Magazine*, 9 January 2017. https://greatergood.berkeley.edu/article/item/five_ways. Accessed 13 June 2023.

———. *Fostering Empathy through Museums*. Rowman & Littlefield, 2016.

Nagaoka, Jerry, et al. "Foundations for Young Adult Success: A Development Framework." *The University of Chicago Consortium on Chicago School Research*, June 2015. *The Wallace Foundation*, https://www.wallacefoundation.org/knowledge-center/pages/foundations-for-young-adult -success.aspx. Accessed 7 June 2023.

"Our Work: Social-Emotional Learning." *The Wallace Foundation*. https://www.wallacefoundation .org/how-we-work/our-work/pages/social-emotional-learning.aspx. Accessed 8 June 2023.

Robinson, Cynthia. "Museums and Emotions." *Journal of Museum Education*, vol. 46, no. 2, 2021, pp. 147–49. *Taylor & Francis Online*. https://www-tandfonline-com.ezp-prod1.hul.harvard.edu/ doi/full/10.1080/10598650.2021.1922987. Accessed 19 Feb. 2023.

Shriver, Timothy P., and Jennifer Buffet. "The Uncommon Core." *Handbook of Social and Emotional Learning: Research and Practice*, edited by Joseph A. Durlak, Guilford Press, 2015, xv–xvi.

"Slow Looking." *Project Zero: CCI Toolkit*, Harvard Graduate School of Education, 2019. *Project Zero*, http://www.pz.harvard.edu/resources/slow-looking-0. Accessed 8 Feb. 2023.

Tishman, Shari. *Slow Looking: The Art and Practice of Learning through Observation*. Routledge, 2018.

"The Twelve Transferable Skills." *UNICEF's Conceptual and Programmatic Framework: Education Section*, United Nations International Children's Emergency Fund, 2022. *UNICEF*, https://www .unicef.org/lac/media/31591/file/The%2012%20Transferable%20Skills.pdf. Accessed 10 Feb. 2023.

Roege, Gayle, and Kyung Hee Kim. "Why We Need Arts Education." *International Association of Empirical Aesthetics*, vol. 31, no. 2, 5 Sept. 2013, pp. 121–30. *Sage Journals*, https://journals -sagepub-com.ezp prod1.hul.harvard.edu/doi/epdf/10.2190/EM.31.2.EOV.1. Accessed 15 Dec. 2022.

Weissberg, Roger P. "Promoting the Social and Emotional Learning of Millions of School Children." *Perspectives on Psychological Science*, vol. 14, no. 1, 2019, pp. 65–69. *Sage Publications*, https://journals.sagepub.com/doi/pdf/10.1177/1745691618817756. Accessed 20 Apr. 2023.

———. "Why Social and Emotional Learning Is Essential for Students." *Edutopia.com*. George Lucas Educational Foundation, 15 February 2016. https://www.edutopia.org/blog/why-sel -essential-for-students. Accessed 28 Apr. 2023.

"What Is Active Listening?" United States Institute of Peace. https://www.usip.org/public -education-new/what-active-listening. Accessed 12 June 2023.

Chapter 3
VRP Activities Toolkit A–Z

This chapter serves as a resource for meaningful museum programming ideas. All of the methods collected here meet the Visitor Response Pedagogies criteria: they are inclusive, work at most museums, and are grounded in transformative and constructivist ideals as well as social-emotional learning. Most of these program ideas are flexible and can be adapted for different-sized spaces and various age groups. A few notes about how this chapter is organized:

1. The activities are listed alphabetically.

2. Appropriate contexts are defined.

3. There is a brief description of each activity with scholarship and origination, if available.

4. The emphasized **Transferable Skills** are listed alphabetically.

5. For most of these activities, no materials are needed beyond paper and pencil (in most museums, art materials are not allowed in gallery/exhibit spaces). If the activity requires additional materials and can be held outside of a gallery space, it is noted in the description of **What It Is**.

6. Art or hands-on activities can always be offered in conjunction with a gallery experience. For some activities, suggestions are made in **Hands-On Extension**. Most of these ideas would require a maker space and additional materials.

7. The **"Museum Highlight!"** sections recognize some of the wonderful programs occurring in museums already.

Happy planning!

Activity: Art Detectives

Would work well for: Any museum visitor at any museum

What It Is: Art Detectives is an activity that relies on Close Looking and honing observational skills. It can be scaffolded for any age range and work at all museums. Sometimes these take the form of a "Seek and Find" activity. Museum educators create "evidence" that provides clues about art or artifacts, and visitors use the clues to locate the pieces. An Art Detective program can take any form and be based on many themes. For example, pieces with a particular theme may be the focus ("joy" or "animals" for example), or visitors can be challenged to find a certain number of "flowers" or other thematic references in a gallery. In a natural history gallery, seeking representations of bird species may be the goal, or mythological references at a history museum. Clues can be playful and open-ended, allowing for personal interpretations. Art Detectives is also a program that can be implemented with a museum educator, with randomly assigned groups or pairings, or as self-guided experiences. Depending on the theme of the program and whether or not the activity is completed and reviewed as a group, the transferable skills reinforced are varied.

Transferable Skills: Close Looking/Observation, Collaboration, Critical Thinking

Hands-On Extension: Printed sheets with reproductions of featured works allow visitors to circle and/or color their discoveries, or draw their own versions of the representations they find.

> **Museum Highlight! The Perez Art Museum Miami** (PAMM) runs a three-part Art Detectives program that promotes critical and timely dialogue between community youth and police. Using art as a catalyst for conversation, PAMM teaching artists work in cooperation with the Miami-Dade Police and Americorps volunteers from Breakthrough Miami through shared art encounters with middle school students. Kids and officers are paired up to engage in close looking activities with various works in the galleries.

Activity: Arts and Letters

Would work well for: Any museum visitor (even if they needed to be read to) at most museums

What It Is: Arts and Letters is a historical term that refers to the combination or union of the arts (visual, performing, etc.) with literature. It is used here to encompass any form of reading program hosted by a museum, preferably using texts that connect in some way to the arts, either specifically to a collection or artistic tradition. The books may also be connected to other museums' themes. Arts and Letters programs may include preschool story times, book clubs for visitors of all ages, or special programs connecting a story or book (historical fiction or fiction) to a particular artist or piece.

Transferable Skills: Active Listening, Close Looking/Observation, Collaboration, Communication, Critical Thinking, Empathy, Self-Awareness

Hands-On Extension: There are numerous art-making extensions for Arts and Letters programs, exploring various mediums and techniques utilized in the stories and/or pieces.

Activity: Awe Walk

Would work well for: Any museum visitor at most museums

What It Is: Awe Walks (sometimes called **Wonder Walks**) have received a lot of attention in the media and have been the subject of several scientific studies examining how walks can encourage people to take fresh looks at what is around them and thereby boost their mental health. Most of these studies focus on walks in nature, but the same premise can be applied to museum spaces. There is ample evidence that walking boosts mood and is good for your overall health, and even fifteen to twenty minutes of walking is beneficial. Museums can structure walks by marking paths/routes with footprints throughout the museum and/or museum grounds. A walking map with prompts (for example, identify something "micro" on which to focus and then on something "macro") would also work, but the idea is not to "guide" too much, rather for people to notice new things in their surroundings while engaging in healthy habits either independently or with others.

Transferable Skills: Close Looking/Observation, Critical Thinking, Self-Awareness

---

Activity: Before and After

Would work well for: Any museum visitor at any museum

What It Is: Before and After is a great activity to use in conjunction with any action-oriented scene, whether that is in a painting, a print image in a book or on a poster, photography, video, or even a scene in a diorama. Visitors engage in Close Looking and imagine what happened right before the scene depicted occurred and what could have happened right afterward. This can be done individually, in pairs, or in groups, and discussions can occur as a large group or as a Think-Pair-Share (see this activity on page 53). Before and After is a flexible activity and can be done in five minutes or less, so it can quickly encourage Close Looking and engagement with a piece and with others.

Transferable Skills: Active Listening, Close Looking/Observation, Collaboration, Communication

Hands-On Extension: Before and After drawing sheets can be reproduced with featured works in between those designated areas (Appendix A).

Activity: Blind Drawing or Blind Contour Drawing

Would work well for: Any museum visitor at any museum

What It Is: Blind Drawing is an exercise in which a participant is instructed by another participant to draw something. It may be an image, an artifact, or a specimen. The participant who is serving as the artist does not see the item. The other participant describes the item without revealing what it is their artist is drawing but provides as many details as possible. This activity is a variation of an art-making activity based in Close Looking called **Blind Contour Drawing**, introduced by Kimon Nicolaides in *The Natural Way to Draw* and popularized by Betty Edwards in *Drawing on the Right Side of the Brain*. The artist draws the contour of a subject without looking at the paper and without lifting the pencil.

Transferable Skills: Active Listening, Close Looking/Observation, Collaboration, Communication, Empathy, Inclusion

Hands-On Extension: This activity only requires paper and pencil, which most galleries allow; however, the activity can be extended using additional drawing materials in an art-making space.

Activity: Blue Light Visualization

Would work well for: Most visitors at museums with applicable works

What It Is: This activity relates to the Color Your Emotions activity in this toolkit and the emerging explorations of the intersection of neuroscience and color. **Blue Light Visualization** falls under the umbrella of mindfulness and meditation, as many healers connect the color blue to relaxation and calm. In museums, pieces that feature the color blue offer opportunities for visitors to connect to the energy or emotion of the color, particularly if there are multiple shades of blue used in one piece. Blue Light Visualization also works well using the sky as the feature, so any museums that have outdoor spaces can offer opportunities for meditative practices and connections to the color blue.

Transferable Skills: Close Looking/Observation, Communication, Self-Awareness

Hands-On Extension:. Visitors enjoy exploring the color blue in any art-making extensions, but particularly using palettes to mix their own shades of blue for painting. "Sky painting" is also a favorite activity, and for some visitors, offering a concrete theme helps their expression.

Activity: Box Breathing

Would work well for: Any museum visitor at any museum

What It Is: Box Breathing is a form of deep breathing popularized by yoga practice. Even the Navy SEALs use box breathing to manage stress. It refers to the fact that a box has four sides, and participants slowly count to four for a total of four times. Participants breathe in for four counts, hold their breath for four counts, exhale for four counts, and pause for four counts. Box breathing has been shown to reduce stress, activate the parasympathetic nervous system, and calm a racing mind. This activity would work as part of any mindfulness practice, but because of the references to boxes and shapes with four sides, it works well in coordination with art or artifacts that include four-sided shapes. Alternatively, this works with triangular shapes and Triangular Breathing with breathing in for three, holding for three, and exhaling for three breaths.

Transferable Skills: Close Looking/Observation, Inclusion, Self-Awareness

Hands-On Extension: Art making based on color field or abstract works is a natural art extension of Box Breathing experiences.

Activity: Breathing

Would work well for: Any museum visitor at any museum

What It Is: There are several specific breathing techniques on the toolkit list, but breathing activities of all kinds work as response activities. Art/artifacts serve as objects of observation and focus. Here is a list of additional breathing techniques: **Alternate Nostril Breathing** involves inhaling through one nostril and exhaling through the other; **Anchor Breathing** is when participants ground themselves heavily like an anchor with heavy breathing; **Bee Breath** is deep breathing with humming on the exhale; **Deep Belly Breathing** requires one hand on the heart and one on the belly; and **Lion's Breath** requires participants to take a deep breath and stick their tongue out on the exhale. Different forms of breathing may correlate well with different topics and/or works.

Transferable Skills: Close Looking/Observation, Self-Awareness

> **Museum Highlight!** The **Aspen Art Museum** in Aspen, Colorado, hosted a collaboration exploring breath as art. Aspen Shakti founder Jayne Gottlieb led participants through a fifty-minute breath and movement experience followed by a sound bath and meditation. Designed for all ages, it included time for socializing over coffee and pastries.

Activity: Cabinet of Curiosities

Would work well for: Any museum visitor at museums that have artifacts that can be touched

What It Is: Cabinets of Curiosities or Cabinets of Wonder emerged in the sixteenth century, and they usually referred to a room filled with one's collection of art and other relics. Many believe them to be the European precursors to museums. Some museums have adopted this history as a style of curation, creating eclectic and diverse displays, sometimes utilizing actual cabinets. As an activity, this refers to exploration and discussion using a collection of diverse artifacts usually surrounding a theme of some sort. If the artifacts can be touched, all the better! Objects serve as the focus for discussion, but the activity also works well in conjunction with some of the others in this Toolkit, such as **Curator Challenge** or **Juxtapose This**.

Transferable Skills: Active Listening, Close Looking/Observation, Critical Thinking

Museum Highlight! The **National Maritime Museum in Sydney, Australia,** hosts a program called **Cabinet of Curiosities** allowing visitors to explore wonderful and curious shipwreck artifacts and maritime archaeology tools in the galleries. The **Hudson River Museum** in Yonkers, New York, hosts a family art program called **Cabinet of Curiosities**, an activity exploring abstraction by repurposing single-use plastics and arranging them in various combinations/colors/shapes inside a clear plastic clamshell box.

Activity: Change One Thing

Would work well for: Most museum visitors at most museums

What It Is: This is a simple but engaging option for dialogical interpretation and guided conversation based in Close Looking. Visitors are asked the question, "If you could change one thing about this work, what would you change?" Responses take conversations down varied paths, from artistic elements such as color, scale, or positive/negative space to topics related to theme/narrative or emotional response. Visitors usually like to play the role of the artist or art critic, and it requires them to think critically and provide reasoning for their preferences or choices.

Transferable Skills: Close Looking/Observation, Communication, Critical Thinking, Self-Awareness

Hands-On Extension: Reproducing masterpieces is an artistic practice dating back centuries when students learned how to become artists by initially working in the style of their teachers. Using **Change One Thing** as a precursor to a "Painting Like a Master" workshop is a fun way for visitors to engage with their inner critic before art making—and perhaps they are encouraged to "Change One Thing" in their own reproductions!

Activity: Color by Number

Would work well for: Any museum visitor at most museums

What It Is: There is ample research connecting the act of **coloring** with mindfulness and other forms of wellness practice. Most agree that not only is the act of coloring fun and peaceful, but it reduces anxiety by bringing order to people's lives. Researchers have also found that coloring is associated with "a number of positive emotions including calmed down, safe, at ease, rested, satisfied" (Koo et al. 2). During the COVID-19 pandemic, the sale of color/paint-by-number kits and coloring books surged. Some museums offer coloring sheets that correspond with featured works, but it is rarely offered as a program even though there is ample evidence that it is a worthwhile activity and one that could easily and inexpensively be implemented at institutions. Certainly, this activity does not need to be limited to a global pandemic, and creating coloring sheets that highlight pieces in a collection along with coloring pencils, cushions, and lap desks/clipboards would appeal to visitors of varying ages and demographics.

Transferable Skills: Close Looking/Observation, Critical Thinking, Empathy, Self-Awareness

Activity: Color Your Emotions

Would work well for: Any museum visitor at any museum

What It Is: Color Your Emotions focuses on color and the connection to emotion. A focus on color serves as a prompt for a group discussion of a piece. Alternatively, the activity can be conducted as a variation on the Personal Response Tour with prepared prompts. Using any image or artifact, visitors connect feelings to colors in particular pieces. This activity works particularly well with contemporary pieces, such as color field works of art, but any piece can serve as a conversation starter about the connection between a color and the emotions it conjures. As an exploratory activity (more like a Personal Response Tour), colors are written or printed on cards and given to individuals or pairs. Visitors have time (fifteen to twenty minutes) to explore galleries or museum spaces to find a representation of the color they are assigned. These may be general in nature (red, blue, etc.) or more specific and wide-ranging (coral, turquoise, etc.). Visitors present their choices to the whole group with a brief discussion on the role of color in the piece and the connections they make between color and feeling.

Transferable Skills: Active Listening, Close Looking/Observation, Communication, Critical Thinking, Empathy, Self-Awareness

Hands-On Extension: A follow-up activity in art making is coloring simple shapes according to labels (sadness, joy, fear, etc.) and the colors with which they are typically associated. This works very well using watercolor paints. This leads to a discussion and opportunity to explore complex emotions (e.g., annoyed, embarrassed, touched, etc.) that may involve mixing colors (appendix B). A great deal of in-depth analysis has been done with some famous masterpieces and their connection to color, such as Van Gogh's *Starry Night*, which, when magnified, displays at least seven different hues of blue. This is another way to approach color analysis.

> **Museum Highlight!** In 2023, students at the **Boise Museum of Art** in Boise, Idaho, explored the artwork of Montana-based artist Willem Volkersz in *The American Dream*. He is known for his neon and paint-by-number style artworks that illustrate his memories of immigrating to the United States. In the art studio, they created works inspired by the artist's pieces.

Activity: Curator Challenge

Would work well for: Most visitors and many museums, particularly those with diverse art and objects (specialty museums, historic homes, etc.)

What It Is: One might argue that the display of art and objects is as interesting as the objects themselves. Introducing visitors to the art of **curation**, or the action or process of selecting, organizing, and looking after the items in a collection or exhibition, is a fun exercise. Facilitators can guide visitors to notice and consider how and why objects are chosen and displayed in certain ways. Nina Simon, in *The Participatory Museum*, writes of visitor curation, "Playing games with objects isn't just high art technique; it can also help visitors construct their own meaning about objects and have some fun while doing so" (161). Participants offer their insights into why objects are displayed in particular ways or imagine how they may redesign exhibits.

Transferable Skills: Close Looking/Observation, Communication, Self-Awareness

Hands-On Extension: Reproductions of art and objects may be offered so visitors can curate their own exhibits, even transferring their ideas into a drawn plan (appendix C), naming their exhibit, and even writing labels.

> **Museum Highlight!** In 2009, the **Powerhouse Museum** in Sydney, Australia, featured an exhibit called *The Odditorium*, putting eighteen strange and fanciful objects on display along with fictitious labels written by author Shaun Tan and schoolchildren. Visitors were allowed to add to the fun by writing their own imaginative (not descriptive) labels for the objects (about which they had no real information). This required visitors to engage deeply with the objects and look for details to support their interpretative stories. The **Idaho Museum of Natural History** in Pocatello, Idaho, hosts a program called "ROAR and Build Your Own Museum," which allows participants to use digital resources to design exhibits and even construct a 3D-printed model of a dinosaur skeleton.

Activity: Daily Schedule

Would work well for: Any museum visitor at any museum; particularly good for art galleries

What It Is: This activity works well for portraiture but could be adapted for other forms of art featuring figures of any kind. Visitors think deeply about the characters portrayed and the lives they may have led. Sharon Vatsky, in *Museum Gallery Activities*, describes using this activity at the Guggenheim Museum with Pierre-Auguste Renoir's *Woman with a Parakeet*. Visitors write out schedules describing the figures' activities and commitments in the morning, afternoon, and evening. They could even just describe their activities orally.

Transferable Skills: Active Listening, Close Looking/Observation, Critical Thinking

Hands-On Extension: Adding a drawing component to this activity in a diary form is a natural extension. Additionally, facilitators may introduce the concept of art journaling in relation to this activity. Art journaling is a visual diary where individuals express their ideas, thoughts, daily activities, experiences, or even memories that pop up using any type of art—sketching, collage, painting, etc.

Activity: Ekphrastic Poetry

Would work well for: Most museum visitors at most museums

What It Is: Ekphrastic Poetry is the meeting of poetry and art. "Ekphrastic" is a Greek expression for "description," and this poetry can focus on actual or imagined works. Group Poetry is described in this toolkit, and that exercise falls under this umbrella; however, there are many other ways to connect visual art with the written word. In fact, sketching thoughts, emotions, and memories often comes more easily than writing them. Some activities—such as the Personal Response Tour—work well to precede writing, sparking connections with or emotional responses to works that lead to written expressions or personal narratives. Other activities that work in concert with **Ekphrastic Poetry** include Before and After or Daily Schedule, which help expand the life of figures in works of art. Artist and writer Lynda Barry, in her book *What It Is*, suggests folding a piece of paper into a grid with six boxes and then drawing a figure from a piece of art in six phases of life to help develop a history or story for that figure.

Transferable Skills: Active Listening, Close Looking/Observation, Collaboration, Communication, Critical Thinking, Empathy, Self-Awareness

Hands-On Extension: There are countless written and visual art extensions for **Ekphrastic Poetry.** After all, words are art in and of themselves. A fun, simple extension is to highlight works at a museum by laminating reproductions or placing the reproductions in acrylic stands on tables where visitors will also find poetry tiles (many versions of poetry tile sets are available for purchase). Visitors work independently or with others to create a poem using the tiles. Taking the activity one step further, visitors write their poems on drawing or watercolor paper and illustrate, creating a new work of art inspired by an existing piece in the museum's collection.

Museum Highlight! The **John and Mable Ringling Museum of Art** in Sarasota, Florida, hosts programs for adults age fifty-five and older through their Lifelong Arts classes. Classes include art making of various mediums, as well as an **Ekphrastic Poetry Bootcamp**, engaging visitors with varied works from the museum's collection and a wide variety of writing and sketching activities.

Activity: Embodiment

Would work well for: Any museum visitor at most museums

What It Is: Embodiment activities address the connections between the physical body and one's cognition or emotional self. In museums, **Embodiment** refers to expressing an emotional understanding with a physical demonstration. Movement is key in embodiment exercises. Tableau Vivant is an example of one kind of embodiment, usually utilized with pieces featuring figures. However, visitors may also imagine being part of a forest of trees or a field of flowers depicted in a work, moving their bodies accordingly. They may act out the words on a page or move their bodies like the hands on a clock, or even respond to sound or music.

Transferable Skills: Close Looking/Observation, Communication, Critical Thinking, Self-Awareness

Activity: Empathy Tours

Would work well for: Any museum visitor at many museums, particularly art and history museums

What It Is: Empathy is a transferable skill reinforced by many of the activities in this toolkit; however, there are museums exploring Empathy specifically with their programming. **Empathy Tours** encourage visitors to practice this skill by naming their feelings and assuming alternate points of view represented in works of art. It does require carefully chosen artifacts or works that evoke emotion or are biographical in some way, such as portraits.

Transferable Skills: Active Listening, Close Looking/Observation, Collaboration, Communication, Critical Thinking, Empathy, Self-Awareness

Museum Highlight! The **Minneapolis Institute of Art** in Minneapolis, Minnesota, developed **Empathy Tours** for middle grades and adults. Their goal was to "create a new kind of tour, one that invites visitors to practice empathy and understand divergent points of view" ("Empathy Tours"). Tours included five to six stops in front of particular works with discussions surrounding assumptions and emotions. They offered opportunities for verbal sharing but also response journaling.

Activity: 5, 4, 3, 2, 1 Breathing

Would work well for: Any museum visitor at most museums

What It Is: 5, 4, 3, 2, 1 is a method of Close Looking. Coupled with breathing, it is also a coping or grounding technique for stress because it takes away focus from something bothering us and focuses us on our surroundings (or on something placed in our surroundings like a piece of art). 5, 4, 3, 2, 1 pairs well with still-life art because it represents objects that we see, touch, hear, smell, and taste in our everyday lives or the lives of artists. Visitors (individually or in small groups, such as family groups) take two to three minutes to closely observe and notice **5** things they see, **4** things they could touch, **3** things they could hear, **2** things they could smell, and **1** thing they could taste. Pencils and notecards with 5, 4, 3, 2, 1 (appendix D) prompts can be available so visitors do not have to try to remember all of their ideas. Groups can share things they see/touch/hear/smell/taste if they desire. Facilitators should also describe how this technique can be used outside of an art experience as a way to help people when they feel anxious. It brings the focus back to the present and one's surroundings and can be paired with a deep breath after each sense.

Transferable Skills: Active Listening, Close Looking/Observation, Collaboration, Communication, Critical Thinking, Empathy, Self-Awareness

Hands-On Extension: This is a fun activity to further explore still-life art in a maker or art space. Tables display a variety of objects that could be used for a still life (plastic fruit, vases, coins, jewelry, fabrics, dishes, plastic flowers/foliage, etc.). Visitors work independently or with a group to consider how still-life art is arranged and use the objects to create a still-life scene. This can be transferred into a sketch or drawing.

Activity: Fortunately, Unfortunately

Would work well for: Any museum visitor at most museums

What It Is: As a classroom teacher, my students loved playing **Fortunately, Unfortunately** in conjunction with the book *Fortunately* written and illustrated by Remy Charlip. Depending on the age of the group, this activity could follow a reading of the book, but it is not necessary. Museum educator and author Sharon Vatsky describes her use of this activity at the Guggenheim Museum in her book *Museum Gallery Activities: A Handbook*. This activity works well with narrative paintings or complex objects. The group is divided in half, and one group starts off with a "Fortunately" statement and the other group follows with an "Unfortunately" statement. For example, group one may start by saying, "Fortunately, it looks like there is plenty to eat" and group two may follow that by saying, "Unfortunately, the fish doesn't look very appetizing." It's a fun way to engage visitors more deeply with a piece and with one another, and it requires no materials.

Transferable Skills: Active Listening, Close Looking/Observation, Collaboration, Communication, Critical Thinking, Empathy, Self-Awareness

---

Activity: Five Senses Immersive Experience

Would work well for: Any museum visitor at most museums

What It Is: Combining **Immersive Sensory Experiences** with art and other objects helps visitors more fully engage with pieces. Depending on gallery limitations and the safety/preservation of the objects, bringing in the sounds, smells, or even tastes associated with a piece heightens learning, memory, and emotional reactions. For example, ocean sounds and the taste of sea salt in combination with a piece like *The Great Wave* by Katsushika Hokusai is a low-cost way to create an immersive experience with a work of art.

Transferable Skills: Active Listening, Close Looking/Observation, Communication, Critical Thinking Empathy, Self-Awareness

> **Museum Highlight!** There are many ways for museums to engage visitors' five senses. The **Denver Art Museum** in Denver, Colorado, has developed a **Sensory Garden**, which is an accessible outdoor space for visitors of all ages to engage with and enjoy plants that evoke the five senses and support the well-being of their visitors. The garden is meant to be actively engaged with and allows visitors to explore the link between creativity and the natural world. The **Tate Britain** partnered with artists to create the **Tate Sensorium**, which brought the museum alive through vision, sound, touch, smell, and taste. For example, while looking at a portrait by Francis Bacon, visitors ate chocolate blended with specific tastes of charcoal, and sea salt, among others. For the painting *Full Stop* by John Latham, viewers used headphones that played specific tones to accompany the painting.

Activity: Geocaching

Would work well for: Any museum visitor at most museums

What It Is: Geocaching is an activity that involves hunting for and finding a hidden object using GPS coordinates. It is a sophisticated treasure hunt or hide-and-seek that may also involve clues. Sometimes it involves taking and/or leaving an object, but it doesn't have to. There are handheld geocaching devices, but there are also websites (Geocaching.com) and apps that visitors can access on their phones if a museum has created an account and a hunt. Geocaching is a creative way to engage visitors with one another and with a museum's collection.

Transferable Skills: Active Listening, Close Looking/Observation, Collaboration, Critical Thinking

Museum Highlight! The **Anchorage Museum** in Anchorage, Alaska, teamed up with Geocaching.com to engage visitors in what they call "citizen science" by participating in a Repeat Photography project (see "Repeat Photography" on this list). In this version, people search for specific geocaches, take a particular photograph at each geocache site, and then digitally share the images.

Activity: Group Poetry

Would work well for: Any museum visitors with some writing skills

What It Is: With **Group Poetry**, small groups are provided paper and pencil and assigned a work of art. After Close Looking, each member of the group writes a thought or question that the subject of the piece may be thinking or feeling. Another approach, if there is no "subject," is asking participants to write down anything they think of when they look at the piece—a detail, a memory, a feeling, etc. After sharing, the group arranges their written lines or questions into a shared poem, however they see fit. Participants move to each piece, and groups share their collective poems with the larger group. This visitor response activity helps develop skills related to Observation, uncertainty, and Collaboration or team building (Chisolm et al. 738) when "participants often realize the differences in perspectives represented by the variation in phrases. . . creating the type of unusual experience that may spark growth" (739).

Transferable Skills: Active Listening, Close Looking/Observation, Collaboration, Communication, Critical Thinking, Empathy, Self-Awareness

Hands-On Extension: Groups could have the opportunity to illustrate their poem, or copies of created poems could be printed for members to keep and illustrate on their own.

Activity: Imagined Conversations

Would work well for: Museum visitors with writing skills or a partner that writes, at most museums

What It Is: This strategy goes by other names—callouts, thought bubbles, etc. The goal of the activity is to imagine what a figure or figures in a piece are thinking or saying. It also works with animal figures. Templates for the thought bubbles used in cartoons are easy to find online, and there are even sticky notes made in various sizes shaped like thought bubbles. Students share their thoughts, bringing life to the featured figures as the various bubbles engage in imagined conversations. Facilitators can provide more parameters, such as asking visitors to pose questions. A printed reproduction of the art piece (poster form) allows visitors to attach their thought bubbles to the piece.

Transferable Skills: Close Looking/Observation, Empathy, Self-Awareness

Hands-On Extension: More opportunities to engage in thought bubble art may be offered by creating printed reproductions of various works with empty conversation bubbles (appendix E). Visitors can choose a piece of art and fill in the bubbles, add color, etc.

Activity: Juxtapose This

Would work well for: Any museum visitor at most museums

What It Is: Juxtaposition is a practice or artistic technique of placing works which may be dissimilar or unrelated side by side or atop one another to create interesting opportunities for comparison and contrast. Curators often refer to juxtaposition as putting works "in conversation" with one another. For example, in one of the most well-known exhibits employing juxtaposition, Fred Wilson's *Mining the Museum* at the Maryland Historical Society, ornate silver pitchers and goblets were displayed alongside iron slave shackles, prompting reflection on history, culture, and race. Any objects can be juxtaposed—linked together by medium, theme, time period, or anything that generates comparisons, contrasts, and conversation.

Transferable Skills: Active Listening, Close/Looking Observation, Communication, Critical Thinking, Empathy, Self-Awareness

Hands-On Extension: A **Curating Workshop** is a unique follow-up to a museum experience employing juxtaposition. Visitors may have their own opportunity, either by using hands-on or digital materials, to create juxtapositions of objects and discuss how curation impacts learning.

> **Museum Highlight!** The **Crystal Bridges Museum of American Art** in Bentonville, Arkansas, hosts a three-day workshop exploring themes of equality, freedom, and social justice through American history. "We the People" juxtaposes works of art with the nation's founding documents, creating conversations and connections.

Activity: Loving-Kindness Meditation

Would work well for: Any museum visitors at most museums

What It Is: Loving-Kindness Meditation is sometimes called "Metta" Meditation. It is a way to cultivate a propensity for kindness by mentally focusing on sending goodwill, kindness, and warmth to others. For a museum experience, facilitators choose a figure of some sort (in a painting, photograph, drawing, book, or sculpture) and engage in Close Looking at the figure. Choosing an expressive figure works best for this exercise. Then the meditation begins, achieved by a series of actions. Participants sit or lie in a comfortable position and bring awareness to their breath. Then participants reflect on the figure, tapping into feelings of empathy or connection. To help with this, participants silently recognize the emotions expressed by the figure—joy, love, pain, sorrow, etc.—and really consider those emotions and the kindness one can show toward that person if encountered. The goal is to rest or linger in those feelings of empathy, kindness, acceptance, etc., for a minute or two. In some cases, facilitators guide participants to repeat mantras—*"May we be happy and contented," "May we feel safe and protected and free from outer and inner harm,"* or *"May we be healthy and whole to whatever degree possible."* The goal as a museum experience is to try to walk a mile in someone else's shoes but also to use those feelings of empathy to draw connections and turn inward to love oneself. The Getty Museum included a Loving-Kindness Meditation in their mindfulness program for teens, using *Man with a Hoe* by Jean-François Millet. A wide variety of artworks may serve as inspiration for a Loving-Kindness Meditation.

Transferable Skills: Active Listening, Close Looking/Observation, Collaboration, Communication, Critical Thinking, Empathy, Self-Awareness

---

Activity: Mind Mapping

Would work well for: Most museum visitors at most museums

What It Is: In classrooms, teachers employ various forms of **Mind Mapping**, allowing students to represent their understanding and conceptualization of ideas in creative ways. These are sometimes called one-pagers, brainstorm maps, web maps, or bubble maps, just to name a few. Mind Mapping is an open-ended, fun way for visitors to record their observations and connections as they look at a piece, and it also offers a chance for them to express their creativity. It serves as a way to record new ideas or as a reflection tool at the end of an experience. One way to begin this activity is to ask visitors to begin with a single word (color, feeling, memory, tangible object) that comes to mind when they look at a piece, and to continue making associations using the piece and their prompt as inspiration. All it takes is a piece of paper, dry writing utensils, and lap desks/clipboards (and perhaps some cushions to offer more comfort).

Transferable Skills: Close Looking/Observation, Critical Thinking, Empathy, Self-Awareness

---

Activity: Mindfulness

Would work well for: Any museum visitor at any museum

What It Is: Mindfulness is finding its way into most museums. They are safe spaces where people can focus on the process of paying more attention to the present. Mindfulness helps people slow their thoughts, be calm, and connect with the moment. It can also help mental health and ease stress. Mindfulness is a type of **meditation** that involves sitting quietly and paying attention to the thoughts, sounds, and feelings of the present moment. The mind will start to wander, but Mindfulness is about acknowledging this and bringing it back to the moment. This practice can take many forms in museums—a daily practice, a program, or more direct instruction such as breathing activities or yoga. These programs can be for children, adults, older people, and health workers. Some museums have started "Mindful Mondays" or other days devoted to Mindfulness programs in museum spaces.

Transferable Skills: Active Listening, Close Looking/Observation, Collaboration, Communication, Critical Thinking, Empathy, Self-Awareness

> **Museum Highlight! Manchester Museum** in the United Kingdom runs drop-in lunchtime Mindfulness sessions, aimed at people who are working in the city but may need a break or reset. They provide lunch and a respite from noise and overstimulation through guided sessions and Close Looking at artwork. The **Mint Museum** in Charlotte, North Carolina, offers a program called Mindful Looking. Visitors preregister to be part of a small group that is led in a meditation session, reflection, or other exercise in concert with a chosen work of art. **The Phillips Collection** in Washington, DC, offers a weekly thirty-minute meditation online, inspired by different works in their collection.

Activity: Multiple Interpretations

Would work well for: Any museum visitor at any museum with some Oral Communication skills

What It Is: Multiple Interpretations encourage social and emotional skills such as dealing with uncertainty, looking at something from different perspectives, and providing evidence for meaning or a point of view. Visitors assemble in front of a piece and break into small groups. Each group is provided a slip of paper that offers an interpretation of the story or circumstances represented in the work of art or artifact. The groups engage in Close Looking together and find evidence for their given interpretation. They present their interpretation and provide the evidence that the group generated. There is no "winning" or correct interpretation. The exercise intends to promote looking at something from many perspectives and helps hone skills related to active and empathetic listening as well as Critical Thinking and Oral Communication by providing supporting details and evidence.

Transferable Skills: Active Listening, Close Looking/Observation, Collaboration, Communication, Critical Thinking, Empathy

Activity: Museum Melodies

Would work well for: Any museum visitor at most museums

What It Is: Music and art are a natural pairing, and juxtaposing music with art and other kinds of objects offers opportunities for reflection, meditation, and discussion. The piece may invite a certain kind of music or sound, such as the featuring of a violin or a waterfall. In specialty museums, sound can give life to artifacts, such as antique cars or other types of machinery. Historic homes can bring life into a room by playing sounds that one may have encountered in a space, such as a kitchen noise, the crackling of a fire, or music played on a record player. Hiring live musicians, inspired by a particular work, to play in a gallery is also inspiring. Consider unique ways to draw visitors into a piece by using music or other sounds.

Transferable Skills: Active Listening, Close Looking/Observation, Communication, Empathy, Self-Awareness

Museum Highlight! The **Anchorage Museum** in Anchorage, Alaska, hosts a summer exploration called "The Sensational World of Sound and Music," which explores the sounds associated with "local soundscapes" as well as Alaskan music. The **Legacy Museum** in Birmingham, Alabama, hosts a program in their Reflection Space, combining music and images to explore issues of racial injustice. The **Wadsworth Atheneum Museum of Art** in Hartford, Connecticut, hosted Haneef Nelson, a jazz trumpet player, and the Birth of the Cool Ensemble, to play while visitors viewed Bob Thompson's painting *Garden of Music*.

Activity: Observe-Connect-Reflect

Would work well for: Any museum visitor at any museum

What It Is: Observe-Connect-Reflect is an activity developed by museum educators at the Cleveland Museum of Art in Cleveland, Ohio, to facilitate conversations between artworks and social-emotional learning; however, the activity is applicable to other kinds of objects. During the "Observe" phase, students share what they see or notice. During the "Connect" phase students make connections between what they saw and their own lives or experiences. During the "Reflect" phase, students consider how the connections they made helped them learn something about themselves.

Transferable Skills: Active Listening, Close Looking/Observation, Communication, Critical Thinking, Empathy, Self-Awareness

Activity: One Word

Would work well for: Any museum visitor at any museum

What It Is: This simple activity sparks conversation about any object. Visitors engage in Close Looking and share a single word that comes to mind. It may be a feeling or place, for example.

Visitors can share their words, with or without explanation. This activity works particularly well when many pieces are being viewed or the group is very large. It is a quick way for participants to personally connect and respond to pieces, but it does not take a lot of time.

Transferable Skills: Close Looking/Observation, Oral Communication

---

Activity: Personal Response Tour

Would work well for: Any museum visitor at any museum with some Oral Communication skills

What It Is: The **Personal Response Tour** is a teaching method that focuses on "personal highlights" (Williams 95) and is initiated by participants blindly choosing a prompt or a guiding question and spending fifteen to twenty minutes exploring museum galleries to find a work that exemplifies or connects in some way to it. For example, a guiding prompt might be *"Find a work of art that sparks joy and reflect on why"* or *"Find a piece that scares you and think about the reasons for your choice."* These guiding questions or prompts are easily scaffolded for the youngest museum visitors (*"Find a painting that makes you feel happy and describe why it makes you happy"*) to teenagers (*"Find a work of art that is most like you. What qualities do you have in common?"*) to adult visitors (*"Which work of art could you share with a friend struggling with depression? Consider the reasons for your choice"*) (99). Participants are encouraged to spend at least five minutes engaged in Close Looking and meaning-making, and when the group reconvenes, the participants become the guides. They move through the galleries to each of their chosen works, and each person shares their prompt and the connection to their chosen work of art. As creator Ray Williams writes, "Inviting museum visitors to share their thoughts and feelings, memories and associations, is both powerful and unexpected" (96).

Transferable Skills: Active Listening, Close Looking/Observation, Collaboration, Communication, Critical Thinking, Empathy, Self-Awareness

---

> **Museum Highlight!** The **John and Mable Ringling Museum of Art** in Sarasota, Florida, works in collaboration with healthcare workers from Sarasota Memorial Health Systems. Museum educators use Personal Response Tours to explore artworks, using prompts that include references to health or experiences related to patients or patient perspectives.

Activity: Photo Bomb

Would work well for: Most museum visitors at most museums

What It Is: Photo Bomb allows visitors to explore the museum and take pictures. There are many ways to do this. Depending on the age of the participants and the resources of the museum, visitors could use their own phone cameras, museum iPads, digital cameras, or Polaroid cameras. Facilitators ask visitors to take photos of anything that captures their attention, an open-ended approach that works well with younger children. A variety of themes would work as well (based on a word/theme, emotion, or color), particularly for older visitors.

Transferable Skills: Close Looking/Observation, Communication, Self-Awareness

Hands-On Extension: This activity is hands-on, but there are numerous ways to display the photos taken by visitors or other art-making opportunities using Polaroids or access to a printer. Additionally, if visitors have access to computers, they can create digital collages.

Museum Highlight! The **Getty Museum** in Los Angeles, California, developed a photography initiative called **Getty Unshuttered**. This program includes a wide range of activities for ages thirteen to nineteen centered on photography, an app for submitting and sharing photos, and resources for teachers. One of the themes was "Reconnection" as students emerged from the COVID-19 pandemic.

Activity: Pick a Side

Would work well for: Most museum visitors at most museums

What It Is: In **Pick a Side**, visitors use multiple transferable skills to evaluate two works that are in close proximity. It is also helpful for the pieces to be of the same or similar medium, although it could work with two completely different styles or mediums. The facilitator poses various statements, and the participants move toward the work that they think best reflets or represents the statements. They can share their reasoning if they like, or they may choose neither work by standing between the two. Some examples of statements include: *This work is beautiful, This work makes me feel happy, This work tells a clear story,* etc.

Transferable Skills: Close Looking/Observation, Communication, Critical Thinking, Self-Awareness

---

Activity: Rapid Fire Response

Would work well for: Any museum visitor at any museum

What It Is: Rapid Fire Response is a technique sometimes referred to as **"And I Noticed."** Visitors in the group line up in front of a work of art or artifact and, using Close Looking skills, share one element or detail that they notice about the piece. The sharing moves quickly down the line, and then the line begins again. Usually, the observations move from list-making or superficial observations (*"There's a woman dressed in blue under the tree"*) to deeper meaning-making or interpretation (*"The woman in blue looks distressed"* or *"The colors in the piece are sort of cold and sad"*). Facilitators may also guide visitors to notice tiny details, such as the dimple in a baby's chin or texture variations in an oil painting. "And I Noticed" de-emphasizes the speed of response, so it works well with smaller groups, while Rapid Fire Response works well with larger groups to keep things moving. Both versions of this activity help visitors with Close Observation, dealing with uncertainty, Communication, connection, and even identity formation (Chisolm et al. 738).

Transferable Skills: Active Listening, Close Looking/Observation, Communication, Critical Thinking, Empathy

---

Activity: Repeat Photography

Would work well for: Any museum visitor at most museums, but particularly in botanical gardens or outdoor spaces

What It Is: Repeat Photography is the practice of taking multiple photographs of the same subject, from the same location, at different times. This is used in natural sciences as comparative evidence for how a natural landscape, for example, changes over time and might be impacted by climate shifts; however, Repeat Photography can be a visually compelling way to document many things. This activity would probably work well with things from the natural world, but it may also work with other kinds of pieces, particularly if another element was introduced into the photo, such as a person returning to the same piece, multiple times, months apart, and taking a selfie.

Transferable Skills: Close Looking/Observation, Communication, Critical Thinking, Empathy, Self-Awareness

---

Activity: See-Think-Wonder

Would work well for: Any museum visitor at any museum

What It Is: See-Think-Wonder was developed by the Harvard Graduate School of Education and Project Zero. It is sometimes referred to as "visible thinking" and is intended to be used in multiple disciplines to support the development of thinking skills and deepen content learning. Participants begin with "See," sharing observations about a work. With "Think" they are asked to back up their observations and interpretations with reasons. Then they "Wonder," reflecting on questions they still have or want to follow up on. This framework is easily utilized with any object and is a quick and meaningful way to generate conversation among museum visitors.

Transferable Skills: Active Listening, Close Looking/Observation, Communication, Critical Thinking, Empathy, Self-Awareness

---

Activity: Sleep Sessions

Would work well for: Museums with meditative spaces or the capacity to host visitors overnight, for visitors old enough to sleep away from home

What It Is: Many museums are quiet meditative spaces, great for practices that lend themselves to healthy sleep. Many of the breathing exercises in this VRP Toolkit, for example, can be utilized for good sleep. Some museums may also be appropriate for sleepovers. Certainly, after-hours access to exhibits offers a different view of a museum's collections, which can be a little haunting, exciting, or beautiful depending on one's perspective! Nighttime tours and explorations of outdoor spaces, such as sculpture gardens or botanical gardens, offer contemplative environments for meditation. Particular objects or artworks offer opportunities for reflection and peace. Depending on the museum, **Sleep Sessions** or sleepovers give visitors a unique and intimate view of a museum space.

Transferable Skills: Close Looking/Observation, Communication, Self-Awareness

> **Museum Highlight!** The **Rubin Museum** in New York City offers a unique sleep experience. The museum, which explores ancient Tibetan art and Buddhist philosophy, hosts an annual "Dream-Over" in which attendees arrive already in their pajamas and sleep beneath a work of art selected—via a self-reflective questionnaire—just for them. All are treated to bedtime stories, lullabies, discussion groups, and, upon waking, a short dream interpretation session with a psychoanalyst. The **Museum of Old and New Art (MONA),** outside Hobart, Tasmania, is a contemporary structure built out of an abandoned sandstone quarry that houses the multimillion-dollar art collection of entrepreneur David Walsh. The property's most striking feature may be the eight individual accommodation "pavilions" in which guests can stay. These cubist structures, built with glass or wood and steel, are their own private galleries filled with famous artworks. Finally, the **Iceland Wilderness Center** gives visitors the chance to find out what it was like to sleep in a bygone era. A former farm close to east Iceland's central highlands, the museum shows how local farmers survived through the centuries and offers guest rooms for interested overnighters looking to experience their way of life, be it in the old farmhouse or the baðstofa—a large common room with close sleeping quarters where families gathered at night to work and tell stories.

Activity: Social Practice Programs

Would work well for: Any museum visitor at any museum

What It Is: Museums are institutions where **social and restorative justice** themes are increasingly addressed. The intersection of **Social Practice** and material culture offers opportunities to engage with the community in conversation surrounding issues such as systemic racism and other forms of racial injustice, or discrete social topics such as immigration or gun violence. Social Justice Programs also examine positive connections, such as how sports or other organized activities are bringing people together. Related to VRPs, choosing a piece as a point of conversation or inspiration is a good way to start, and if the artist or creator is local, that brings opportunities to engage in the community more deeply.

Transferable Skills: Active Listening, Close Looking/Observation, Communication, Critical Thinking, Empathy, Self-Awareness

Museum Highlight! The **Guggenheim Museum** in New York City serves as a great model for social justice programs in museums. The Guggenheim **Social Practice Initiative** collaborates with artists who work within the field of socially engaged art. Their programs aim to connect art with the community, including a piece by Shaun Leonardo (and a related program) called *Primitive Games*, where four "divided" groups are invited to debate current issues, such as gun violence, without using words. Another program, . . . *circle through New York*, creates connections through social and material exchange between areas normally separated by factors like cultural or economic boundaries, using a piece by Lenka Clayton and Jon Rubin as inspiration.

Activity: Sound Baths

Would work well for: Any museum visitor at any museum

What It Is: A **Sound Bath** is a meditative experience when attendees are "bathed" in sound waves from different sources such as gongs, singing bowls, chimes, tuning forks, or even humming or chanting from the human voice. Sound baths help individuals achieve deeper states of relaxation and healing as usually heart rates and blood pressure decrease. Sound baths and Close Looking at works of art are a natural pairing, with numerous ways to employ this activity.

Transferable Skills: Active Listening, Close Looking/Observation, Self-Awareness

Hands-On Extension: Art-making activities related to sound allow visitors to bring the meditative practice to their own homes and lives. Chimes are very easy to create with various pipes, bells, or natural materials.

Museum Highlight! The **Denver Botanic Gardens** in Denver, Colorado, offers several Singing Bowl Meditations using crystal and Himalayan singing bowls, as well as an Om Gong, to help people find deep relaxation and inner stillness in concert with the natural environment.

Activity: Soundscapes

Would work well for: Any museum visitor at most museums

What It Is: Sound is another way to activate the senses and connect to emotion. Music is one way to do this, as we explored in Museum Melodies; however, curated sound is also impactful. Either as part of an exhibit through a sound system, or with the use of phone apps and QR codes, visitors can listen to contextual sounds—the hum of traffic on a busy street, the sound of breaking waves on a beach, or animal vocalizations—that bring works of art to life and offer an alternative to the expected audio tours offered at museums. As a facilitated experience, immersive **Soundscapes** followed by guided conversation are inclusive in that they provide a common language that visitors can explore in connection to works.

Transferable Skills: Active Listening, Close Looking/Observation, Communication, Critical Thinking, Empathy, Self-Awareness

---

Activity: Staff Suggestions

Would work well for: Most museum visitors at most museums

What It Is: Perhaps you have seen **Staff Suggestions** or Staff Picks written on cards and displayed at bookstores and libraries. Staff members identify authors, illustrators, and genres, providing details that influenced their selection. There are multiple ways to adapt this practice in museums, with staff identifying favorite exhibits or objects, features that influence them, stories of personal connections and resonation, and notes of interest about the piece/medium/artist. Putting a "Staff Picks" board in an entrance gallery introduces a museum's collections and provides an overview of what visitors are preparing to see. Additionally, the suggestions may steer visitors a particular way if a staff member's pick description inspires them. Finally, "Staff Suggestions" can easily be adapted to "Visitor Picks," and facilitators can offer visitors the chance to fill out cards about their favorite pieces, sharing similar information, at the conclusion of their visits.

Transferable Skills: Close Looking/Observation, Communication, Critical Thinking, Empathy, Self-Awareness

---

Activity: Tableau Vivant

Would work well for: Any museum visitor at any museum

What It Is: Tableau Vivant means "living pictures" in French, and it was an extremely popular form of entertainment between 1830 and 1920. A form of Embodiment, this activity allows participants to mimic the positions and shapes of figures or characters in a piece of art, displayed on an artifact, or described in a piece of writing. Participants copy the poses, postures, and gestures of the figures. Participants freeze in their positions, and the museum facilitator can help others with their poses, if needed.

Transferable Skills: Close Looking/Observation, Collaboration, Communication, Self-Awareness

Hands-On Extension: Additional opportunities for playing with posing may be offered in a maker space, where props and/or costumes can help make particular pieces come to life.

Museum Highlight! The **Getty Museum** in Los Angeles, California, started a popular trend at many museums involving a digital version of **Tableau Vivant** that spread to social media platforms like Instagram and Twitter. People started recreating artistic masterpieces in modern, creative ways and sharing them along with a museum hashtag. This trend offers "an embodied experience of art that inherently celebrates excess, drama, irony, and play" (Smith).

Activity: Tour by Theme

Would work well for: Any museum visitor at most museums

What It Is: Larger museums can sometimes be overwhelming. **Tours by Theme**, either self-guided or facilitator-led, narrow the collections for overwhelmed or time-limited visitors. A theme such as "Flora and Fauna," for example, narrows the number of pieces to visit, and visitors can be led to pieces that feature nature or follow a guide to particular pieces. It is important to pick themes that are accessible to all visitors.

Transferable Skills: Active Listening, Close Looking/Observation, Collaboration, Communication, Critical Thinking

Museum Highlight! The **John and Mable Ringling Museum of Art** in Sarasota, Florida, offers self-guided tours by theme ("Animals" is a popular one for younger visitors) by highlighting pieces on ExploRINGS, which are laminated clues on rings that visitors can pick up and carry with them. The **James Museum of Western and Wildlife Art** in Saint Petersburg, Florida, offers guides highlighting themes, such as "Mountains" and "Sky," in their collection. Offering multiple themes encourages repeat visits and breaks down the content/collections of larger museums into multiple self-guided visits.

Activity: Twenty Questions

Would work well for: Any museum visitor at any museum

What It Is: A tried-and-true game, **Twenty Questions** can be used as a fun, open-ended museum experience, either with groups or individuals. Visitors can ask facilitators Twenty Questions about a piece either to guess the artist, medium, time period, title, etc., or just to learn details about a particular piece. Visitors can be put into groups in more of a "competition" to learn as much as they can about a work, and then present the piece and see who obtained the most accurate information. Twenty Questions can also be printed on cards and serve as prompts. This works well with objects/artifacts, with questions such as "How was this object used?" or "What words would you use to describe this object?" The best learning outcome of Twenty Questions is the reinforcement that most art leaves us with more questions than answers!

Transferable Skills: Active Listening, Close Looking/Observation, Collaboration, Communication, Critical Thinking

> **Museum Highlight!** The **Anchorage Museum** in Anchorage, Alaska, created "Twenty Questions to Ask Any Object." As they describe, their deck of twenty questions can be used with any kind of object at the museum—a sculpture, a canoe, a photograph, a typewriter, or a parka. Using Close Looking, visitors are encouraged to pull a question from the deck and consider their response, working either independently or collaboratively.

Activity: Think-Pair-Share

Would work well for: Any museum visitor at any museum

What It Is: Think-Pair-Share is a collaborative learning strategy first developed by Frank Lyman at the University of Maryland. I used this daily in my classroom and called it "Turn and Talk," another way it is commonly known. This is a method to generate discussion and participation among visitors, but in a low-risk way since many people do not like sharing in front of a larger group. Visitors consider the question posed by a facilitator, then pair up with another visitor and share their perspectives. Turn and Talk works in basically the same way, except that once the question is posed, visitors immediately turn and talk through it with someone in their vicinity, usually only for a minute or so. This strategy works well for museum settings because most of the time, groups are smaller and interactions are brief.

Transferable Skills: Close Looking/Observation, Collaboration, Communication, Critical Thinking

Activity: Tools of the Artist

Would work well for: Any museum visitor at most museums

What It Is: Sharon Vatsky, a museum educator at the Guggenheim Museum in New York City, describes this activity as an opportunity for participants to make connections between materials and art/artifacts. Facilitators bring in tools used to create whatever piece is featured, such as a paintbrush or range of brushes, sculpting tools, or other materials. Vatsky describes bringing a turkey baster on wooden sticks to an activity featuring Jackson Pollock's drip painting *Alchemy* in her book *Museum Gallery Activities*. Visitors discuss how the tools contribute to the piece, such as which paintbrushes made which strokes.

Transferable Skills: Close Looking/Observation, Communication, Critical Thinking

Hands-On Extension: Depending on the tools, facilitators could offer opportunities for visitors to experiment using them. For example, if the discussion centered on using various paintbrushes to create particular brushstrokes in a work, offering opportunities to paint and experiment with the brushes in an art-making space would be a valuable extension of the in-gallery experience.

Activity: Upside-Down Drawing

Would work well for: Most museum visitors at many museums, especially art museums

What It Is: Artist and author Betty Edwards calls **Upside-Down Drawing** "an exercise that reduces mental conflict" (530). Our brains are confused when images or writing are inverted, and a different side of the brain is forced to take over until what we see is righted. There are neurological benefits to these cognitive shifts. Reproductions of museum works (portraits work particularly well) can be inverted, and visitors use Close Looking to draw the image as they see it with pencil on paper. Only at the completion of the sketches should participants revert both their drawings and the original to compare what they perceived to what is reality.

Transferable Skills: Close Looking/Observation, Communication, Critical Thinking, Self-Awareness

---

Activity: Viewfinders

Would work well for: Any museum visitor at any museum

What It Is: A **Viewfinder** is a tool that enables artists to frame or crop a particular scene to arrange their composition (appendix F). They help visitors engage in Close Looking/Observation by focusing on one small area at a time rather than looking at the entirety of something. Participants can describe what they see through the finder in detail with a Think-Pair-Share or Turn and Talk. Visitors can move their Viewfinder and see the work from different perspectives. Viewfinders can be square, rectangular, or other creative shapes.

Transferable Skills: Active Listening, Close Looking/Observation, Collaboration, Communication

Hands-On Extension: Drawing scenes as they are framed by the Viewfinder is a fun extension.

Activity: Viewpoints

Would work well for: Any museum visitor at any museum, but works well with large-scale pieces

What It Is: Visitors find a different position to view an object rather than just standing directly in front of it. This works best with works of art/sculpture, but it could be done with other types of artifacts. This method is particularly effective with large-scale works, such as outdoor pieces or architecture. Visitors can sit or lie down in various positions to change their view of the object, engage in Close Looking, and share their observations.

Transferable Skills: Close Looking/Observation, Communication, Critical Thinking, Self-Awareness

Hands-On Extension: Sketching the viewpoint of the work is a fun art-making extension of this activity.

Activity: Visual Journaling

Would work well for: Any museum with most age groups

What It Is: Visual Journaling is a reflective process that involves exploring concepts, ideas, and thoughts visually in order to understand and create personal meaning. It is an expressive visual art process that involves the exploration and application of mixed media to the pages of a notebook or sketchbook. A visual journal could be a collection of mixed-media pages with free-form expression, or a deep dive into connecting the arts with your innermost feelings and reflections of the world. As a museum experience, facilitators can lead visitors in initiating a visual recording of pieces in their collections—through sketching a section of a painting or recording colors they notice using colored pencils, or writing about their emotional responses to pieces. They may draw a flower or leaf they notice outside of the museum, or cut out part of a pamphlet or handout describing an exhibit. A museum collection is a wonderful way to initiate this type of creative, observational practice.

Transferable Skills: Close Looking/Observation, Communication, Critical Thinking, Empathy, Self-Awareness

Hands-On Extension: Moving an introductory program in Visual Journaling to an art or maker space allows for further exploration of artistic mediums beyond sketching with pencils. The use of watercolor or other paints, collage materials, etc., can be explored along with sample journals for inspiration.

> **Museum Highlight!** The **Georgia O'Keeffe Museum** in Santa Fe, New Mexico, offers an online course for ages twelve and up called "Introduction to Visual Journaling." It encourages and instructs on the use of mixed media (doodles, paintings, sketches, clippings, collages, collected items) to create an artistic journal. The museum also encourages parents and children to take the course together.

Activity: Visual Thinking Strategies (VTS)

Would work well for: Any museum with any age but works best with artwork and artifacts

What It Is: VTS is a strategy to facilitate complex conversations using an object (usually a piece of art) as the focus of the conversation. It is based on the research of Abigail Housen and the Five Stages of Aesthetic Development and the work of museum educator Philip Yenawine. It is centered on three questions: *What's going on in this picture? What do you see that makes you say that?* and *What more can you find?* Reframing and paraphrasing responses are also part of the facilitation of VTS. Online training in VTS facilitation is offered at vtshome.org.

Transferable Skills: Active Listening, Close Looking/Observation, Collaboration, Communication, Critical Thinking, Empathy, Self-Awareness

> **Museum Highlight!** The **Wild Center** in Tupper Lake, New York, partners with VTS, creating workshops and toolkits for science museum educators and classroom teachers to improve their ability to observe, think, listen, and communicate within a science context. They use live specimens, artwork, or even habitat dioramas to facilitate VTS conversations with student visitors.

Activity: Yoga

Would work well for: Any museum visitor at most museums

What It Is: Yoga is a spiritual, physical, and mental practice that has origins in India over five thousand years ago. The Sanskrit roots of the word, "yujir" and "vuj," mean "joining" and "connection/coming together." Yoga in museums is growing in popularity, offering beauty and meditative, safe spaces for community practice. Yoga classes may be inspired by a particular piece—connecting poses to images such as "tree" pose, "warrior" pose, or "sun salutations." In these cases, visitors move from piece to piece, find space, engage in Close Looking, and then hold a particular pose. Other classes may focus on one piece, and visitors set up for a longer practice. Some museums, such as the Brooklyn Museum, hold classes for three to four hundred people at a time, setting up in a large atrium. Yoga also works well in sculpture gardens. However the activity is organized, yoga and museums are a great match if the museum has the space.

Transferable Skills: Close Looking/Observation, Self-Awareness

Museum Highlight! The **Rubin Museum** in New York uses its collection of art from the Tibetan plateau, the Himalayas, India, and other neighboring regions in concert with yoga classes for thirty to forty people. Their Yoga Connections class includes a discussion about how yoga connects to art in the museum. A yoga teacher and a museum guide select a piece to inspire discussion about its origins, yoga, philosophies related to mind and body, and visual representations.

Works Cited

Barry, Lynda. *What It Is*. Drawn and Quarterly: Illustrated edition, 2008.

Chisolm, Margaret, et al. "Transformative Learning in the Art Museum: A Methods Review." *Family Medicine*, vol. 52, no. 10, Nov.–Dec. 2020, pp. 736–40. *STFM Journals*, https://journals.stfm.org/familymedicine/2020/november-december/kelly-hedrick-2020-0242/. Accessed 11 Jan. 2023.

Edwards, Betty. *Drawing on the Right Side of the Brain*. TarcherPerigee, 2012.

"Empathy Tours." Minneapolis Institute of Art.

Housen, Abigail. "Art Viewing and Aesthetic Development: Designing for the Viewer." *Visual Understanding in Education: Visual Thinking Strategies*, 2007. *Visual Thinking Strategies*, https://vtshome.org/wp-content/uploads/ 2016/08/2Housen-Art-Viewing-.pdf. Accessed 17 Jan. 2023.

———. "Three Methods for Understanding Museum Audiences." *Museum Studies Journal*, Spring/Summer 1987. *Visual Thinking Strategies*, https://vtshome.org/wp-content/uploads/2016/08/6-3MethodsforMuseumAudiences.pdf. Accessed 6 Jan. 2023.

Housen, Abigail, and Philip Yenawine. "Understanding the Basics." *Visual Thinking Strategies*. Updated by Madison Brookshire, Aug. 2018. *Arts Integration*, https://www.artsintegration.net/uploads/1/2/2/6/12265539/bp_understanding_ the_basics_.pdf. Accessed 16 Jan. 2023.

Koo, Malcolm, et al. "Coloring Activities for Anxiety Reduction and Mood Improvement in Taiwanese Community-Dwelling Older Adults: A Randomized Controlled Study." *Evidence-Based Complementary and Alternative Medicine*, 2020, pp. 1–6. https://doi.org/10.1155/2020/6964737. Accessed 12 July 2023.

Nicolaides, Kimon. *The Natural Way to Draw: A Working Plan for Art Study*. Harper Design, 1990.

Reynolds, Gretchen. "An 'Awe Walk' Might Do Wonders for Your Well-Being." *New York Times*, 1 October 2020.

Simon, Nina. *The Participatory Museum*, Santa Cruz, CA, Museum 2.0, 2010.

Smith, William S. "Tableau Vivants Are Giving Us Life during the Pandemic." *Art in America*, 8 May 2020. https://www.artnews.com/art-in-america/columns/tableaux-vivants-replicate -art-masterpieces-during-covid-19-quarantine-1202686492/. Accessed 29 June 2023.

Vatsky, Sharon. *Museum Gallery Activities: A Handbook*. American Alliance of Museums, 2018.

Williams, Ray. "Honoring the Personal Response: A Strategy for Serving the Public Hunger for Connection." *Journal of Museum Education*, vol. 35, no. 1, Spring 2010, pp. 93–102. *JSTOR*, https://www-jstor-org.ezp-prod1.hul.harvard.edu/stable/25701644. Accessed 8 Feb.

Chapter 4

Evoking Exalted Attention

Museum Objects and VRP Activities

The job of a museum educator is not necessarily to be a scholarly expert in everything. It is, however, the job of an educator to be knowledgeable and recognize pieces in a museum collection that will resonate with visitors—pieces that may inspire awe or curiosity. Historian and Harvard professor Stephen Greenblatt describes this as the resonance and wonder of objects, or their ability to elicit contemplation and emotion in a viewer. As he writes, resonance refers to "the power of the displayed object to reach out beyond formal boundaries to a larger world, to evoke in the viewer the complex, dynamic forces from which it has emerged" and wonder as "the power of the displayed object to stop the viewer in [their] tracks to convey an arresting sense of uniqueness, to evoke an exalted attention" (Greenblatt 42). Museum educators help highlight objects of awe beyond the recognized or obvious masterpieces that might otherwise be missed.

Museum educators at museums of all genres are doing interesting things that inspire visitors to wonder and reflect on objects in their collections. While doing research for this text, I scoured the websites of museums state by state and continent by continent, looking at their collections and their programming. For most, I was able to anticipate the types of experiences that I would find on their events calendars, depending on the type of museum. Children's museums largely offer hands-on, experiential play or art-making workshops with various themes. Science museums lead tours and experiences related to particular concepts, often aligning themselves with educational standards. Art museums lead guided tours of preselected (usually their most well-known) pieces, offering insight into the artists, their inspirations, and their mediums. Historic home guides lead visitor tours highlighting the home's most interesting artifacts and describing how various rooms were used, including the occasional story about its inhabitants. Many museums offer maker workshops and art classes. These activities are valuable and enjoyable, and many visitors expect these offerings when they visit particular institutions. An art museum that never offered a gallery walk or lecture on a featured artist would miss an opportunity to share its expertise. That said, there is space for additional approaches that offer visitors alternative experiences. Visitor Response Pedagogies highlight opportunities for people to experience a museum's treasures in ways that may resonate with more visitors and have social and emotional value, replacing or adding to existing museum programming.

Recently, I visited a museum with an impressive private collection of glass art. Currently, this particular museum does not have an educator on staff but instead relies on community volunteers for tours and programs, many of whom were previously teachers or artists. The educator with whom I spoke kindly shared her tour plan for a recent group of seventh-grade students. She playfully asked the students to pose as detectives tasked with figuring out the messages and motivations of particular pieces and artists in the collection. Students used close looking and critical thinking (great transferable skills!) to share their guesses, and then the guide revealed the real content or actual motivations and background of each artist and piece. The weakness of this format is that it reinforces that there are correct and incorrect guesses or conclusions. If the goal of a tour is knowledge transfer or a curatorial narrative, then I prefer it to be fully didactic instead of giving the illusion that visitors are able to construct their own meaning before being told, "Great guesses. But actually, you're wrong . . ." For this tour, the guide had created a lesson plan which included about six pages of learning objectives and information related to the pieces. There were no state-standard connections for this tour, but much factual content was covered. In fact, the guide took the students to sixteen pieces during a one-hour tour, repeating the same format for each piece. When I asked whether or not she thought content related to sixteen pieces was a lot to cover, particularly for twelve- and thirteen-year-olds, she said she did not think it was too much. She added that she actually covered more than that because she likes to talk about additional pieces that are not necessarily on the planned tour but that they pass as they move from room to room. When I mentioned that I often use a singular piece during a museum experience, she was flabbergasted and said that she thinks educators and visitors would be very disappointed if they visited and the program only examined a few pieces, let alone a singular piece.

This may be true! I enjoy informational tours and learning about the special pieces in museums' collections. There are definitely visitors like me who go to museums to do the same and ones who have this expectation. Visitor Response Pedagogies are not intended to replace these kinds of didactic experiences but instead are intended to supplement or offer alternative learning experiences using pieces in a collection. The goals of these learning experiences are different (as we have covered in earlier chapters). For many, particularly those who do not visit museums often or who think museums are "not for them," VRPs expand the types of experiences museums offer and the realms of learning to the self and community.

Most VRP activities in chapter 3's toolkit only require a single object. There are exceptions (for example, the Cabinet of Curiosities or the Personal Response Tour when visitors find multiple pieces that resonate with them), but many of the activities use one work as an object of interest or focus. Carefully choosing this one object, therefore, is important. Just like Visitor Response Pedagogies' wide-ranging applicability to various museums, the objects that can serve as focal points for activities are broad as well. Art means different things to different people, but I define it in wide terms. Art includes paintings, sculptures, works on paper, and photography—but also music, textiles, fashion, artifacts, specimens, and other types of displays such as dioramas or videos. Literature and all types of performance art such as dance or spoken word also may serve as inspiration for an activity. Rather than a particular type of art or artifact, what makes a piece "good" for Visitor Response Pedagogies are specific descriptors or criteria.

Criteria for Choosing Objects for VRPs

The more multidimensional the aesthetic, the more we open up ways for visitors to be impacted. As Magsamen and Ross write in *Your Brain on Art*, "You are literally changed, on a cellular level, by aesthetics . . . all stimuli that we encounter—visual, auditory, somatosensory, gustatory, olfactory—change the structure and function of cells within our brains and bodies" (99). Choosing the right stimuli is important in eliciting responses from visitors and maximizing the opportunities for cognitive and social-emotional growth. There are six descriptors to consider when choosing an object or objects for Visitor Response Pedagogies, and they are inspired by Philip Yenawine's identified criteria for using pieces in conjunction with Visual Thinking Strategies; however, there are additional considerations. Objects used with Visitor Response Pedagogies should be: accessible, ambiguous, compelling, culturally relevant, multisensorial, and narrative. In the best case, facilitators will use pieces that inhabit all of these criteria. Let's look at each of these elements:

Accessible

Objects should be **accessible**, easily understood, and appreciated by diverse visitors. There should be a point of "entry" or "connection" for people. An example of a piece that may not be accessible is one that uses a lot of religious symbolism such as a cross or a painting with biblical references. It does not mean that a religious or spiritual piece would never work, but something that is deeply rooted in religious practice and relies upon knowledge of a particular religion would not be accessible to a wide range of visitors.

Ambiguous

Objects that are **ambiguous** are ones that are open to more than one interpretation and may be understood in more than one way. The use or depiction may be unclear or inexact, depending on the interpreter's prior knowledge and point of view. A popular example of ambiguity in visual art is the *Mona Lisa*, perhaps specifically due to her smile. Historians and laypeople alike have varying interpretations of her curious (contented? lonely?) expression, and as a result the work is ambiguous, lending itself to many interpretations. Another definition of ambiguous in relation to art refers to images where two different visual interpretations may be seen, depending on one's angle or point of view, or simply the way one's brain takes in the information. An object can often be ambiguous. I participated in an activity with an unusual vessel as the focus. We engaged in Close Looking, imagining its uses, and I am not sure anyone in the group was correct in their assumptions. The ambiguity of the object made for a fascinating discussion.

Compelling

All of these descriptors are tied to one another, and one can easily argue that if an image is ambiguous, it is therefore more compelling. **Compelling** pieces are ones that evoke interest or attention in powerful ways. There is something captivating about them. A compelling object, for example, may utilize interesting materials (such as mirrors), be ornately decorated or detailed, create confusion, or include powerful imagery that invokes a sense of awe or other strong emotional response.

Culturally Relevant

Pieces that are **culturally relevant** reflect a wide variety of beliefs, values, and customs. Objects and images that are culturally relevant also may connect to important current issues around the world—immigration or social justice, for example—and allow for deeper discussion and exploration. An oil painting from the 1700s of a European castle may not be relevant (or accessible . . . ambiguous . . . or compelling . . .) to a wide range of visitors.

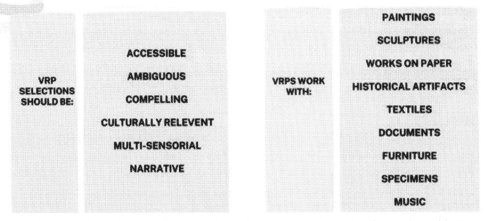

CONSIDERATIONS WHEN SELECTING WORKS FOR VISITOR RESPONSE PEDAGOGIES

| VRP SELECTIONS SHOULD BE: | ACCESSIBLE AMBIGUOUS COMPELLING CULTURALLY RELEVENT MULTI-SENSORIAL NARRATIVE | VRPS WORK WITH: | PAINTINGS SCULPTURES WORKS ON PAPER HISTORICAL ARTIFACTS TEXTILES DOCUMENTS FURNITURE SPECIMENS MUSIC |

Figure 4.1. Considerations when selecting works for visitor response pedagogies. *Source:* Ames Morton-Winter, M.A.ED., ALM.

Multisensorial

Pieces that are **multisensorial** arouse more than one of the five physiological senses, and there is research supporting that learning is enhanced if more than one sense is evoked when taking in new information (Thyssen and Grosvenor). In other words, if a piece has an interesting texture, it may evoke the sense of touch or a tactile connection. If a piece makes a sound, such as an instrument or a clock, that adds to its interest. Integration of our sensory modalities enhances the learning process.

Narrative

Objects or pieces that are **narrative** imply a story. For example, a butterfly specimen may be interesting and beautiful, but as a stand-alone object, it does not tell a particular story (although I am sure there are plenty of visitors who could create a narrative for a butterfly specimen!). If, however, the butterfly specimen is part of a habitat diorama, or put into conversation with another object such as a pesticide bottle, it allows multiple narratives and avenues for interpretation. Narrative objects offer opportunities for imaginative or associated interpretations.

Using VRPs in Different Kinds of Museums

In chapter one, I shared the International Council of Museums' newly adopted definition of a museum, describing it as an institution "in the service of society that researches, collects, conserves, interprets and exhibits tangible and intangible heritage. . . . [O]pen to the public, accessible and inclusive, museums foster diversity and sustainability" ("Museum Definition"). As educators, we must think about ways to meet the parameters of this definition in the experiences we offer our visitors. This is required of the wide range of institutions that fall under the museum umbrella. Because many objects work with Visitor Response Pedagogies, the activities can be used in many types of museums, and responsive activities contribute to the aspiration to serve the public, be accessible, be inclusive, and foster diversity and sustainability.

In this section, we examine the range of institutions that are considered museums and provide examples of some VRP activities that can be utilized at these museums. To be clear, I created sample plans utilizing real museums and real exhibits, but these plans are illustrative and are not plans created or implemented by the institutions I highlight.

Art Museums

Art museums are spaces, sometimes referred to as galleries, that display different kinds of art. Museums may have privately or publicly owned collections. Some museums are accessible, offering free admission (at least on certain days), and some rely on generating revenue to keep their doors open. Encyclopedic museums are large, often nationally funded, that cover a wide time frame and range of cultures and styles of art, and some art museums display smaller collections or specialize in a particular type of art, such as contemporary art.

The activities in the VRP Toolkit are easily utilized at most large and mid-sized encyclopedic museums, given the wide range of art and artifacts at an educator's disposal. Additionally, smaller specialty art museums are well suited for many VRPs, including Breathing and Mindfulness, explorations of color and connection to emotion, and Viewfinder activities, just to name a few.

Sample Plan

VRP Activity: Tools of the Artist

Object/Location: *Landscape at Saint-Remy* by Vincent van Gogh at the Indianapolis Museum of Art, Indianapolis, Indiana

SEL/Transferable Skills: Close Looking/Observation, Communication, Critical Thinking

Materials: a variety of paintbrushes

Activity: Visitors engage in Close Looking at van Gogh's piece, focusing on brushstrokes and the texture/movement the brushes create. After a discussion, the facilitator shares various paintbrushes of different sizes, shapes, and textures. These can be passed around with discussion surrounding which brushes may have been responsible for brushstrokes in the painting.

Wrap-Up: A follow-up art activity allows visitors to experiment with the brushes in creating different strokes, shapes, etc

Botanical Gardens

Botanical gardens are institutions dedicated to a living collection of plants, and they offer wonderful opportunities for learning beyond didactic tours. Some botanical gardens, such as the Marie Selby Botanical Gardens in Sarasota, Florida, incorporate art regularly into their displays, usually with some sort of botanical connection. Other gardens, such as the Bayfront Gardens at the John and Mable Ringling Museum of Art in Sarasota, Florida, incorporate sculptures and

Sample Plan

VRP Activity: Nature-Inspired Yoga

Object/Location: Marie Selby Botanical Gardens in Sarasota, Florida

SEL/Transferable Skills: Active Listening, Close Looking/Observation, Collaboration, Communication, Critical Thinking, Empathy

Materials: yoga mat

Activity: Selby Gardens has several areas away from general visitors and foot traffic appropriate for yoga sessions. A nature-inspired yoga works for any age group but would likely resonate well with younger visitors. Using the outdoor surroundings as inspiration, either a certified yoga instructor or yoga-capable volunteer leads visitors in yoga poses such as Sun Salutation, Tree Pose, Frog Pose, Seed Pose, Butterfly Pose, Locus Pose, Lotus Pose, Cobra Pose . . . there are many from which to choose!

Wrap-Up: Visitors offer suggestions for other poses inspired by their surroundings.

statues into their garden displays, including Mable Ringling's Rose Garden. Some botanical gardens focus solely on the plants. No matter the type of botanical garden, such museums have peaceful spaces for reconnection to the beauty of our natural world, offer opportunities for Close Looking and reflection, and are perfect for activities that support well-being. Plants serve as objects as well, and they can be put into communication with other items. Drawing activities work well at botanical gardens, as well as Meditation, Yoga, and other Mindfulness experiences. Botanical gardens also offer more physical space than indoor museums, so larger groups can assemble and spread out for activities. Botanical gardens are important community spaces with numerous avenues to support community wellness through VRPs and other programs.

Children's Museums

My earliest experience working with and in museums was at a children's museum. Children's museums are a bit different than most museums as they tend to be play-oriented spaces, highly interactive and stimulating, often with no "collection" in the traditional sense. They provide fun and engaging activities and manipulatives, stimulate curiosity, and motivate learning. Often their exhibits focus on a theme (sometimes tied to educational standards) and offer creative ways to explore that topic. Topics can be wide, such as the human body, or narrow, such as pollination. Generally speaking, children's museums are intended for younger children, usually up to age ten. Additionally, a children's museum's "collection" tends to be interactive and tactile, so exhibits are created with durability and safety in mind. Many children's museums utilize technology to share information and capture the attention of their young visitors, offering chances to exercise the mind as well as the body by incorporating play spaces, climbing structures, and other physical activities.

Sample Plan

VRP Activity: 5, 4, 3, 2, 1 Close Looking/Grounding Technique

Object/Location: *Happy Camper* Exhibit, Please Touch Museum, Philadelphia, Pennsylvania

SEL/Transferable Skills: Active Listening, Close Looking/Observation, Communication, Critical Thinking, Self-Awareness

Materials: none

Activity: In this permanent exhibit at Please Touch, young visitors use the exhibit's manipulatives to imagine camping in the great outdoors, including activities such as building fires, roasting marshmallows, observing forest animals, and gazing at a twinkling night sky. This imaginative play is brought to life using the five senses, enabling a sensory experience. Facilitators ask visitors to find a comfortable place to relax, take in their surroundings, and observe five things they can see, four things they can touch, three things they can hear, two things they can touch, and one thing they could taste. This not only brings the environment to life but also provides a calming or grounding technique that can be paired with deep breathing. Visitors may share aloud or at the end of a quiet minute, or they may collaborate with family members. There are many ways to employ this activity in an imaginary play space.

Wrap-Up: Depending on the age of the group, facilitators explain how the activity can be used anywhere, anytime, to soothe nerves or reduce anxiety.

Children's museums also provide opportunities to engage with objects via Close Looking, Collaboration, Critical Thinking, and other transferable skills. Depending on the themes being explored at a museum, objects of all kinds can serve as a focus for responsive activities and hands-on extensions. Thematic rooms that focus on natural history, music, or other cultural themes may provide objects for contemplation and study. Many children's museums have outdoor spaces where larger groups can engage in Breathing activities or Yoga practice. Many discussion techniques, such as Visual Thinking Strategies, Think-Pair-Share, Fortunately/Unfortunately, or Rapid-Fire Response, are particularly enjoyed by children. Although nontraditional and play oriented, children's museums provide ample opportunities to offer activities that support social-emotional learning and wellness.

Cultural Centers

Cultural centers also fall under the umbrella of museums since they promote culture and arts. They are wonderful organizations for responsive activities because they are usually community based with connections to the diaspora and historical context that they represent. In this way, a more diverse range of visitors is often reflected. Cultural centers also host many events, including community meetings, lectures, plays, art exhibits, and celebrations. Because of this, visitors that go to cultural centers often have a connection of some kind—either as part of the culture represented or as a member of the community—to the space and mission. As cultural centers

Sample Plan

VRP Activity: Loving-Kindness Meditation

Object/Location: Class photo from the first class at Jefferson School—African American Heritage Center, Charlottesville, Virginia

SEL/Transferable Skills: Close Looking/Observation, Communication, Critical Thinking, Empathy, Self-Awareness

Materials: none

Activity: Facilitators ask visitors to focus on one figure/face from the school photograph and try to connect to that person, observing their posture, expression, age, gender, etc., and tap into feelings of empathy and connection, imagining what the person is experiencing at the moment of the photo—nervousness, trepidation, pride, empowerment, fear, etc. Visitors are encouraged to linger in those emotions. Depending on the age of the visitors, facilitators may lead them to repeat several mantras—*"May we feel safe and protected and free from outer and inner harm," "May we be happy and contented"*...

host performances, VRPs that work with performance art as inspiration may work well. Musical instruments or lyrics, historical documents, artifacts, local art, historical photographs of the community . . . all of these work in conjunction with VRPs and exercise transferable skills such as Active Listening, Collaboration, and Empathy, thereby enhancing community well-being.

Historic House Museums

Historic House Museums are homes of historic significance that have been preserved, mostly displaying the original placement of items (furnishings, for example) and the way the items were used. They aim to reflect the memory of the people who once resided there and the role they played in society and/or the community. Historic homes often have complicated histories, depending on their location and the inhabitants. Plantation homes, for example, are grand examples of historic house museums, but their beauty relied on the labor of enslaved people. Many historic homes grapple with issues of the past, contemporary relevancy, and authenticity. However, if a historic home is committed to an authentic narrative, it can play an important, evolving role in the community and initiate important conversations.

Filled with objects for reflection, as well as outdoor gardens and gathering spaces, VRPs work with historic house visitors of all kinds. Activities that ask visitors to imagine the lives of the people that lived there—Daily Schedule, for example—work well with images of the home's inhabitants. Object-oriented activities such as Cabinet of Curiosities or Curator Challenge work well at historic house museums, which are filled with *things*. Five Senses Immersion activities also aid visitors in imagining the sights, sounds, smells, tastes, and feels of life in the home. Arts and Letters activities that connect visitors with stories from the time period of the home are also successful. Multiple Interpretations allow for looking at an object from the different perspectives of those who inhabited the property, including staff. It is also interesting

Sample Plan

VRP Activity: Daily Schedule

Object/Historic Home: Monticello in Charlottesville, Virginia

SEL/Transferable Skills: Active Listening, Close Looking/Observation, Collaboration, Communication, Critical Thinking, Empathy

Materials: Morning/Afternoon/Evening schedule printed on two sides of a sheet of paper, one to imagine the daily schedule of Thomas Jefferson and/or his wife and one to imagine the daily schedule of the enslaved people who ran the home, provided on a clipboard with a pencil

Activity: During the tour of the home, visitors are invited to make notes using the two-sided daily schedule provided to them, one for the home's owners and one for the home's enslaved staff. Using the objects and artifacts as clues to the daily activities of each of those groups, visitors step into the shoes of those who lived in the home, as well as those who worked in the home and lived on Mulberry Row. By considering how the home and its objects were used during the course of a day, and by inserting their uses into the framework of a schedule, the objects come to life—particularly when visitors consider the uses of objects by both the owners and the staff.

Wrap-Up: Visitors have the opportunity to share their schedules

to consider exploratory activities such as Personal Response Tours when visitors connect to a piece through a prompt, or Photo Bomb where visitors use cameras and take pictures of items that capture their interest. Historic house museums offer myriad ways for responsive and reflective activities from which visitors can learn about people from the past and about those in their present community.

History Museums

History museums devote their spaces to telling the stories of a particular time or place. They usually include art, artifacts, and other objects that unfold chronologically. Many different kinds of artifacts work together to tell a story. Perhaps because the nature of a history museum is to educate visitors on a particular time and place, history museums tend to lean particularly didactic in their offerings; however, the range of artifacts makes them perfect for responsive activities. Portraiture and old photographs work well with activities such as Daily Schedule and Before and After. Old documents and writings work well with Visual Thinking Strategies. Art Detectives allow visitors to seek knowledge on their own. Embodiment activities encourage visitors to try to inhabit the time and place of a room or event. Arts and Letters activities draw connections between fiction and nonfiction stories of a time and place. These are just a few examples.

Sample Plan

VRP Activity: Juxtapose This

Object/Location: The National Museum of African American History and Culture, Washington, DC

SEL/Transferable Skills: Active Listening, Close Looking/Observation, Communication, Critical Thinking, Empathy, Self-Awareness

Materials: blank cards and pencils, or cards/printouts with objects from the museum's collection and their locations

Activity: Any objects can be juxtaposed, linked together by medium, theme, or time period; objects generate comparisons, contrasts, and conversation. To begin, facilitators choose one of the many displays that group different kinds of objects together by theme to point out how curators create small collections within the larger collection to tell part of the story. After this discussion, there are several ways to approach this activity. Visitors are given fifteen to twenty minutes to explore the galleries, making note of two or more objects that, as curators, they may choose to juxtapose in a display. Depending on the age/demographics of the group, facilitators may choose to guide the visitors a bit more, offering a ring with printed cards featuring arts and artifacts in the museum and their locations. Visitors locate and view the pieces, choosing two or more items from the highlighted pieces. This can also be done with a printed sheet of highlighted objects provided to each visitor, and they can circle their choices.

Wrap-Up: Visitors reconvene and, if they like, share the two to three pieces that they would choose to "juxtapose" in their own hypothetical exhibit. This initiates interesting conversations about the stories the objects tell and/or contrasts between them.

Libraries and Library Exhibitions

Libraries share some of the opportunities and some of the challenges that museums face in terms of relevancy and community connection. Many libraries lean into their roles of not only lending books but also serving as community spaces—hosting lectures and performances, providing services such as technology or financial education and support, and offering programming. Libraries also accommodate exhibits, and some have designated gallery spaces for permanent or rotating installations. This past fall, I attended a wonderful exhibit hosted by the University of Virginia Libraries, *Visions of Progress, Portraits of Dignity, Style, and Racial Uplift*, featuring century-old portraits of Black Virginians. In 2021, the New York Public Library opened its first permanent collection called the Polonsky Exhibition of the New York Public Library's Treasures, featuring manuscripts, artworks, letters, images, videos, and recordings. The diverse collections at libraries, as well as the well-established reputation of libraries as spaces for community gatherings, make them wonderful places to implement VRPs. Arts and Letters programs are obvious choices, but depending on the available space and themes of the exhibits, many activities in the VRP Toolkit will work for library exhibitions.

Natural History Museums

Natural history museums are scientific institutions with collections from the natural world that include current and historical records and examples of animals, plants, fungi, ecosystems, geology, paleontology, and climatology, among other subjects. Natural history museums focus on observational study over experimentation, and in this way, VRPs are a natural fit for the many objects and artifacts found in these museums. Choosing the right object is particularly important. Natural history museums are logical settings to tackle planetary challenges, such as climate change, using objects to spark conversation. For this reason, some of the VRPs that open dialogue would work particularly well—One Word or Fortunately/Unfortunately, for example. Using specimens such as insects or birds, or habitat displays, are fun to pair with Color by Number activities. Blind Contour Drawing is an enjoyable activity with plant life or rock formations. Many natural history museums have habitat enclosures, such as the Butterfly Pavilion at the Smithsonian's National Museums of Natural History. Some natural history museums explore biodiversity and organize by ecosystem, using live specimens and/or dioramas. VRP activities such as Tableau Vivant, or a Five Senses Immersion Activity, may work well with these spaces. Art Detectives is another fun activity to engage visitors in Close Looking and exploratory discovery. Finally, natural history museums often embrace outdoor spaces where visitors can go on an Awe Walk and where various Mindfulness experiences can be held.

Sample Plan

VRP Activity: Color by Number

Object/Location: "World of Shells" at The Fernbank Museum of Natural History, Atlanta, Georgia

SEL/Transferable Skills: Close Looking/Observation, Critical Thinking, Empathy, Self-Awareness

Materials: coloring sheet with drawn reproductions of shells on view, clipboards, colored pencil sets

Activity: Taking advantage of Fernbank's vast display of both shells from the coast of Georgia as well as samples from around the world, visitors of all ages engage in this self-paced coloring activity that encourages people to slow down, engage in close looking, and recognize the beauty of the natural world. Visitors are offered a coloring sheet that highlights several specimens on view. This can be offered in the style of a "Color by Number" or allow for visitors to color as they wish. The locations of the shells might be indicated or facilitators can build in a "Seek and Find" element to the coloring sheets (please note* it is also important to consider the position of the shells for viewing—if there are shells that easily viewed, allow space for sitting off to the side, out of the way of other visitors, for example, those shells might be preferable to highlight. Or a special exhibit related to the coloring sheets might be created in an appropriate space).

Niche Museums

Niche museums are museums with a singular focus and are dedicated to niche collections of any kind—they may also be considered art museums, history museums, or science museums. Some favorite niche museums I have visited or intend to visit include the Edgar Allan Poe Museum and the Museum of Sleep, both in Richmond, Virginia; Etta's Lunchbox Café and Museum in New Plymouth, Ohio; Velveteria: The Museums of Velvet Paintings in Portland, Oregon; the National Museum of Roller Skating in Lincoln, Nebraska; the Robert C. Williams Paper Museum in Atlanta, Georgia; the International Spy Museum in Washington, DC; and the Typewriter Museum in Trani, Italy. Niche museums are fun and play an important role in documenting artistic, cultural, and historical trends, as well as showcasing artifacts that might not otherwise find their way into fine art museums or larger institutions. Often niche museums are connected in some way to their communities—Edgar Allan Poe was from Virginia, and the inventor of the typewriter was Italian, for example. Niche museums, however, often struggle for funding and visitorship. Responsive, wide-ranging programming can help with that! In terms of VRPs at niche museums, space is often the biggest consideration; however, niche museums offer unique cultural artifacts for contemplation that are often less intimidating and more relatable than a fine art masterpiece.

Sample Plan

VRP Activity: Tour by Theme—"Strings"

Object/Location: Museum of Musical Instruments (MIM) in Phoenix, Arizona

SEL/Transferable Skills: Active Listening, Close Looking/Observation, Collaboration, Communication, Critical Thinking

Materials: printed Tour by Theme guide (or digital guide on iPads or available to download)

Activity: The MIM is the world's largest global musical instrument museum with around sixteen thousand musical instruments and two hundred thousand square feet of space. This is an atypical niche museum because of its size, and for some visitors, such a museum might be overwhelming. Self-guided Tours by Theme are one option that allows visitors to create a "museum within the museum" and narrow the scope. Facilitators offer a printed or digital guide that leads visitors to instruments connected by a theme—"Strings" are the example used here—but the possibilities for themes are many. This can be conducted in a Seek and Find format, or in a more self-guided tour format. String instruments that represent a variety of time periods, cultures, sounds, etc., are listed in a logical fashion for exploring and viewing. For some, this gives permission to visitors to focus on particular pieces, perhaps to save others for another visit or time. Multiple Tours by Theme can be created simultaneously, allowing visitors to pick what interests them, or new Tour Themes can be introduced and rotated to create new reasons to visit again.

Wrap-Up: Self-guided activities like Tour by Theme are fun to follow up with a Visitor Suggestions activity. This allows for feedback from visitors who explore the galleries on their own and are not part of a timed program or group. Visitors write about a particular instrument they enjoyed seeing/hearing/learning about and fill out a Suggestions card that allows for written and/or drawn responses. These are posted on a "Suggestions Board" for future visitors.

Performance Art/Performing Art Centers

Performing art centers deserve to be included under the umbrella of museum spaces. They are multiuse performance spaces such as stages for concerts and theaters to screen films. Performing arts centers are used for a wide range of artistic platforms, including musicals, dance, and plays/theater, and they often hold art exhibits in nonperformance areas. They are also community spaces to host speakers and other gatherings. Visitor Response Pedagogies are easily employed with performance arts and offer unique opportunities for meaningful experiences that enhance social-emotional learning. They also usually offer large physical spaces that accommodate families, schools, or large tour groups. Some examples of VRP activities that work well are Embodiment exercises, when visitors can move to featured music or dance; Breathing activities in concert with music; Five Senses Immersive Experiences in conjunction with sets for musicals and plays; Group Poetry in response to a performance; any discussion techniques, such as Think-Pair-Share or One Word; or even a hands-on activity such as Visual Journaling. The options for use of VRPs with performance art are wide open.

Sample Plan

VRP Activity: Group Poetry

Object/Location: *Every Ocean Hughes: River* at the Whitney Museum of American Art in New York City, New York (March 2023)

SEL/Transferable Skills: Active Listening, Close Looking/Observation, Collaboration, Communication, Critical Thinking, Empathy, Self-Awareness

Materials: Paper strips (1–2 per visitor) and a pencil

Activity: This performance imagines mythological crossings through song, text, choreographed movement, and set design. Hughes merges the trope of descending into the underworld—a recurring motif in ancient mythologies—with a transcultural frame of the "crossing." It addresses the closely entwined themes of legacy, loss, and inheritance through its cast of characters, which includes two protagonists, chorus-like figures, and a banjo player. Visitors are provided with one to two strips of paper and a pencil, and they are asked to write responses or questions inspired by the performance. They are encouraged not to compose technical, "practical" questions or observations (e.g., *Where did you learn to play banjo?*) but instead to address meaning, themes, wonderings, and emotions experienced during the performance.

Wrap-Up: There are different ways to utilize the sentence strips. If there is a predetermined group of visitors, it can reassemble following the performance and arrange sentences in any way they see fit, creating a Group Poem about the performance. They may even give it a title and share it orally. If the group is large, multiple groups can be formed. Another approach is to offer the activity to any visitor attending the performance. Visitors can pick up an activity packet containing sentence strips, a pencil, and directions. A magnet board is set up outside the gallery or theater to create an interactive activity. Visitors add their sentences to the board after the performance, posting them with small magnets and allowing visitors to arrange and rearrange what is shared into various poems.

Science Museums

Science museums aim to promote scientific literacy for visitors of all ages. Most science museums are organized around specific concepts—physics, states of matter, etc.—and are sometimes tied to educational standards. Gone are the days of static scientific displays and detailed explanatory text. Most science museums have embraced learning through experiential, hands-on activities, demonstrative exhibits, technology interactives, and visuals. It is common to see educators set up carts or tables for closer examination of specimens or artifacts, and programming tends to be thematic and exploratory. Using the museums' rich collection of images and objects, VRPs can add to science museums' programming range. For example, many science museums have planetariums offering education about galaxies near and far; however, planetariums also offer dark, peaceful, climate-controlled environments where visitors can engage in numerous Mindfulness activities—Meditation and Breathing exercises—that they can take into their everyday lives. Similar to natural history museums, current events, and issues such as global warming can be

Sample Plan

VRP Activity: Awe Walk

Object/Location: *Infinite Amazement: The Mirror Maze* at the Museum of Science+Industry in Chicago, Illinois

SEL/Transferable Skills: Close Looking/Observation, Critical Thinking, Self-Awareness

Materials: none

Activity: Visitors engage in an exploratory walk through this unique exhibit, which by design inspires awe! The mirror maze itself is a pattern, combining several characteristics of geometric patterns: repetition, symmetry, and tessellation using equilateral triangles. These triangles fit together without any gaps or overlaps, creating a tessellation. Mirrored surfaces all around reflect the pattern so that it repeats and appears infinite. Visitors may be offered a guide with reflective questions.

Wrap-Up: There are other activities that can be used in conjunction with an Awe Walk. Rapid Fire Response would work well for this exhibit, with visitors placed in a line within it and taking turns sharing observations or personal responses. One Word is another great wrap-up, with visitors sharing one word that reflects their experience walking the maze.

addressed through Close Looking activities (Juxtapose This, for example) as well as discussion prompts such as One Word or facilitated sessions using VTS. Awe Walks are also appropriate for science museums, as well as Personal Response Tours that utilize questions in alignment with the scientific themes—for example, *"Find an image that makes you think about the future"* or *"Find an object that reminds you of a childhood discovery."* There are also numerous opportunities for Five Senses Immersion Activities.

Sculpture Gardens

A sculpture garden or sculpture park is an outdoor space that includes the presentation of sculpture, usually larger in scale and permanent, and a park of landscaped surroundings. Sometimes these are part of a museum space—many large art museums include sculpture gardens, for example—but some are part of parks or are stand-alone features. Some of the most well-known include the Tehran Museum of Contemporary Art Sculpture Garden in Tehran, Iran, the Esplanade Ernest-Cormier in Montreal, Quebec, the Storm King Art Center in New Windsor, New York, and the Glenstone Museum in Potomac, Maryland. The opportunities for responsive activities in these spaces are many, as there are no space limitations and being outdoors allows for many Mindfulness practices. For example, Yoga, Breathing, and Awe Walks are VPRs well-suited to sculpture gardens. Viewpoints is another appropriate VRP activity at sculpture gardens, allowing visitors to look at large works from different perspectives. Viewfinders also allow visitors to focus on different parts of large-scale pieces. The Glenstone Museum leans into these opportunities, offering programs such as "I Love My Leaf: Formalism, Mindfulness, and Plant Identification," which uses Close Looking at plants to slow the mind. They also offer a program called "Reading

Sample Plan

VRP Activity: Viewpoints

Object/Location: The Sculpture Garden at the Hirschhorn Museum, Washington, DC

SEL/Transferable Skills: Close Looking/Observation, Communication, Critical Thinking, Self-Awareness

Materials: clipboards with paper, pencils

Activity: Visitors choose from one of the thirty sculptures in the Hirschhorn's outdoor garden and find a comfortable position to view it. Facilitators encourage visitors to find different, creative positions for viewing rather than just standing directly in front of their chosen piece. They may choose to sit at the rear of the object, very far away, or very close up, or, if able, visitors can lie down and look up at their piece. This activity can be done in several ways. One idea is to allow visitors to explore, choose a piece, engage in five minutes of Close Looking and Observation in a unique position, and then join up again with their group to share orally. Another idea is to give visitors clipboards with paper, pencils, and additional time. Visitors sketch their chosen sculpture from their vantage points.

Wrap-Up: This activity may be concluded with One Word—asking visitors to share one word to describe their object or experience—to serve as a whole group wrap-up.

Colors: Color Theory 101," which examines how color can change the effect of an artwork as well as a viewer's emotions toward the work.

Visitor Response Pedagogies and their related activities work in most museum settings and with most visitors. Choosing impactful objects and finding the right activity for the object is an important part of the process and may require some trial and error. It is also important to consider the appropriate activity for the type of museum, its space, and the audience in creating memorable experiences.

Works Cited

Adams, Geraldine. "ICOM Unveils New Museum Definition." *Museums Association*, 31 July 2019. https://www.museumsassociation.org/museums-journal/news/2019/07/31072019-icom-reveals-updated-museum-definition/#. Accessed 30 May 2023.

Greenblatt, Stephen. "Resonance and Wonder." *The Poetics and Politics of Museum Display,* edited by Ivan Karp and Steven D. Lavine, Smithsonian Institution Press, 1991, pp. 42–54.

Magsamen, Susan, and Ivy Ross. *Your Brain on Art: How the Arts Transform Us*. Random House, 2023.

"Museum Definition." *International Council of Museums.* 24 Aug. 2022. com.museum/en/resources/standards-guidelines/museum-definition/. Accessed 10 August 2023.

Thyssen, Geert, and Ian Grosvenor. "Learning to Make Sense: Interdisciplinary Perspectives on Sensory Education and Embodied Enculturation." *The Senses and Society*, vol. 14, no. 2, 2019, pp. 119–30. *Taylor & Francis*, https://www.tandfonline.com/doi/epdf/10.1080/17458927.2019.1621487. Accessed 26 July 2023.

Chapter 5

Together We Can Do Great Things

The Importance of Productive Partnering

I appreciate the saying, "I can do things you cannot, you can do things I cannot; together we can do great things" (supposedly Mother Teresa said this when she received the Presidential Medal of Freedom in 1985, but she was, in fact, misquoted!). Regardless, the sentiment is key. Despite the acknowledgment that museums need to be accessible to more diverse populations and establish themselves as essential community spaces, there is more to accomplish. An integral step in achieving these objectives is to collaborate with nonprofit organizations and other community groups to attract guests to the museum and identify needs. Additionally, conducting outreach to take programming off-site to various locations and communities is also valuable. Productive partnering results in more inclusive and robust education, and with Visitor Response Pedagogies in particular, having diverse perspectives enriches many of the experiences and contributes to the development of social-emotional learning.

In both partnering and outreach, museums need to explore creative ways to reach new populations—aging individuals, neurodiverse individuals, neighborhood schools and school groups, homework clubs, sports teams, art clubs, and service organizations are just some of the avenues museums can pursue to widen their net. By working in collaboration, museums can offer varied experiences and benefit from the organization's relationships, expertise, and structures already in place. Let's look at some examples of museum partnerships as well as some examples of museum outreach.

Partnerships

By definition, partnerships refer to the collaboration of two or more organizations working together toward mutual benefit. Museums can work in partnership with other museums or community organizations toward several shared goals: creating a sense of community, celebrating a particular heritage or history, the increasing and diversifying visitorship . . . the list is long. For the purposes of this text, partnerships refer to working with groups to bring visitors into the museum for a program or experience. Additionally, partnerships indicate repeat visits, perhaps with the same group of individuals for a multivisit program, or perhaps multiple groups from an organization on subsequent visits. Either way, the experiences are not one-time events, and the relationship is ongoing.

Museums can work in partnership with other museums with shared goals. The goals may include increasing visitorship by providing a ticket that allows purchasers access to several museums for one entry price. These types of programs have been implemented on a large scale through organizations such as the North American Reciprocal Museum (NARM) Association, which allows members of one participating museum to enter over thirteen hundred museums with a membership. Many states have created similar organizations at the state level. For example, the Iowa Museum Association builds bridges between Iowa's more than four hundred muse-ums "in their efforts to expand access and engage their communities . . . promoting sustainable practices, offering mentorship, facilitating professional development, and providing access to shared knowledge and resources" (Lung 148). Much of the shared access is in the form of digi-tized collections, particularly of primary sources, educational lesson plans, and other resources. Moreover, there are ways to partner even more locally, within cities or towns. If museums are within walking distance of one another, they may offer a shared ticket at a discounted price to see both museums.

Other partnerships may be formed out of goals related to mission. In "Museum Highlights" in chapter 3, I mentioned the Getty Museum's partnership with artworxLA in creating a multipart Mindfulness program for teens as they started to resocialize after the COVID-19 pandemic. The Getty Museum identified a need, designed an approach to using its collection to support well-being, and found a partner with an organization that had an ongoing relationship with a teen group that would benefit from such a program. The Getty's program serves as an excellent example of a community partnership.

Sometimes multiple museums and organizations work together around a shared goal. The Studio Museum in Harlem's community partnerships program is a unique example of mission-orientated partnering centered on social justice initiatives. It includes "organizations that focus on houselessness and housing insecurity, targeted criminalization and reentry from incarceration, health and mental health access, and fostering safe LGBTQ spaces" ("Community Partnerships"). Some of these organizations include the Ali Forney Center, which serves LGBTQ houseless youth, AHRC Fisher Day Center, which supports individuals in Harlem with intellectual and develop-mental disabilities, and Fortune Society at Castle Gardens, which supports successful reentry from incarceration. With each of these organizations, staffs work together to create safe spaces both within and outside the museum by "fostering inclusive creative spaces and inquiry-driven critical dialogue in support of social justice through centering the works of artists of African descent" ("Community Partnerships"). Although some of their work is outreach oriented, the programs are connected to works of art in the Studio Museum's permanent collection.

Other partnerships may focus on particular populations. Museums work in partnership with local organizations and their staff who have expertise in serving specific groups, which helps to broaden the museum's audience. These types of partnerships allow for a greater variety of visitors and enhance the relationship with those communities. In addition, many organizations have infrastructure to support visits such as transportation for its members, additional staff, and other special accommodations needed to support the experience. For example, museums rec-ognize the power of art and museum spaces for individuals with autism. The Spectrum Project collaborated with the San Diego Natural History Museum (the Nat) to create a framework that museums could adopt when hosting visitors with autism spectrum disorder (ASD). This ranged from changing overhead lighting to reconfiguring groups and seating arrangements and offering sensory items such as hard candy for sucking or fidgets to keep hands busy. The Nat worked in partnership with an advisory group representing the Social Stories Spectrum Project (funded by the Institute of Museum and Library Services). Moreover, once the framework was developed, this particular group of ASD young adults participated in organized trips to visit seven museums in the Balboa Park area of San Diego, where they used photography to document their experiences and create visual cues for future visitors with ASD.

Other examples of partnerships focused on a particular population include museums connecting with visitors with dementia. As safe spaces that foster wellness, museums all over the world are partnering with organizations to create impactful, meaningful programs for older adults with memory disorders. For example, the Museum of Modern Art (MoMA) in New York City hosts a program called "Meet Me at MoMA," which focuses on interacting with and creating art. The Royal Albert Memorial Museum and Art Gallery in Exeter in the United Kingdom hosts "Living Each Season," which facilitates interactions and art-making sessions that focus on the present moment. When working with specific populations, the partnering organization offers suggestions about appropriate materials, lighting and room arrangement, timing, and even colors and decoration of spaces.

Schools represent another important partnership. Later in this chapter, I address how to implement responsive activities for local school systems and tie them into educational standards; however, there are other kinds of close partnerships forged under the umbrella of schools and education, namely with museum schools. The National Association of Museum Schools (of which there are over fifty across the country) defines museum schools as schools that "prioritize the building of partnerships with museums to engage students in learning opportunities that are interactive, engaging, and meaningful. Museum Schools, housed in urban and rural settings across the US, successfully serve students that represent a variety of cultural, geographic, and economic experiences" ("Who We Are"). There is an effort to create these schools with diversity in mind, and although many of them tend to be in affluent areas, they are becoming increasingly diverse, with the average number of museum school students receiving free and reduced lunch nationwide at 55 percent ("What is a Museum School"). There is wide variation between museum schools, and no overarching requirements. However, the 2022 *Trendswatch* newsletter, published by the American Alliance of Museums (AAM), anticipates that the number of museum schools will increase exponentially as public schools seek the support of community infrastructure, predicting more than two thousand by the year 2040. The relationship goes both ways, however, and the AAM determined museums as central to a community's infrastructure, with education for children listed as the museum's most important pillar. They recognize four kinds of museum schools: schools using local museums as classrooms, schools creating museums, schools hosted on museum campuses, and museums creating or cocreating a school.

Many museum schools partner with local organizations, namely museums of all kinds, zoos, theaters, and other learning centers, to provide enriching experiences for their students. Field trips are plentiful for museum schools, although outreach plays into this equation as well with traveling exhibits and visits from museum professionals in the classroom. Museum schools tend to be grounded in project-based learning, and students often hold their own exhibit nights when they synthesize something they have learned over a period of time.

There are also museum schools that create museum spaces as part of their curriculums. The Webb School in Claremont, California, has created a full museum for grades 9-12, engaging students in the process of curating collections, creating exhibits, and conducting research. The Raymond M. Alf Museum of Paleontology is a result of this process, and it is now accredited by the American Alliance of Museums. There is value in this process, even on a small scale. My own students often created "classroom museums" when they studied other cultures in social studies. In the VRP Activities Toolkit in chapter 3, there are several activities related to the creation and critical analysis of exhibiting objects, including Cabinet of Curiosities, Curator Challenge, and Juxtapose This.

Some museum schools are housed in museums, such as the Grand Rapids Public Museum School, a school for sixth through twelfth graders that uses place-based design thinking and the museum context to create unique learning experiences. Place-based learning "immerses students in local heritage, culture, ecology, landscapes, opportunities, and experiences as a foundation for the study of language arts, mathematics, social studies, science, and other subjects" (Carlton). The Grand Rapids Public Museum School curriculum aims to inspire passionate curiosity, nurture creative problem-solving skills, cultivate critical thinking, and encourage innovation.

It is relevant to note that in making the case for museums as essential community infrastructure, the other four pillars identified by the American Alliance of Museums include recognizing museums as community spaces that support livable communities for our elders, mental health, emergency response in the face of disasters, and a human-centered culture of sustainability. With all five of the pillars identified by the AAM, Visitor Response Pedagogies play a role either directly (as with education for our children, elder communities, and mental health) or indirectly by providing support through appropriate VRP activities. For example, during Hurricane Ian in September 2022, The John and Mable Ringling Museum of Art in Sarasota, Florida, turned their attention to the community's needs, running online education programming and assembling art kits to deliver to donation centers for students out of school. Once the museum reopened, the education staff provided respite for parents with art-making sessions, offering water and snacks as well as charging stations for people's electronic devices. VRP activities, such as Breathing and Mindfulness, could also add to a museum's emergency responses in cases like Hurricane Ian.

Outreach

There is a lot of overlap between partnerships and outreach programs, and one might argue that all outreach programs require partnerships. For this text, I am using "outreach" to describe a program that represents the museum but travels outside of the museum space. Outreach programs expand museum work to reach communities that tend to be excluded, underrepresented, or marginalized. Outreach can involve and invite these individuals into the fold of the museum and hopefully, eventually, into the museum itself. Outreach addresses the inaccessibility of particular spaces and services for some individuals. They can be beneficial for schools with limitations such as location, cost, or class size that prevent them from taking students on field trips. School groups can make use of the museum's collection and expertise through these programs. There may be groups, such as those who are hospitalized, that cannot travel. There are other outreach programs that "fill a gap" in time, such as after-school groups or childcare organizations. Whatever the type of program or population, outreach is an important way for a museum to gain access to new future museumgoers and to contribute to the community.

Museums traveling to schools are a great example of outreach programming. These instances may take the form of a particular experience, a curricular connection, a "traveling exhibit," or a "culture kit" that assembles examples of art and artifacts representing a particular time, place, and/or cultural group. Field trips are becoming more challenging for public schools. Many school districts have strict rules about field trips. For example, most districts require that an entire grade must be included in a field trip, and for some schools that may be 100–150 students or more. Then there are issues of supervision and cost, as well as thematic limitations as some districts require a direct link to educational standards (we will address this at the end of the chapter).

One outreach option is for museums to create "traveling exhibits" and send museum educators or volunteers to classrooms with art and other objects. Research has shown that the impact of "traveling exhibits" is significant, but only 17 percent of museums (even museums that engage in outreach) have created traveling exhibits as part of their programs ("2022 Annual Performance Report"). Dr. Angela Eckhoff, professor of teaching and learning at Old Dominion University, studied the outcomes of a multiyear exploratory arts outreach program that worked with thirty-one rural elementary and middle schools in the American South that previously had no involvement with any art museums or art galleries mainly due to the costs and distance associated with the closest museums. Working in collaboration, the teachers, museums, and artists created a curriculum, a process that Eckhoff identifies as key to a successful outreach program. She writes that it is "important to carefully consider design and intentionality behind outreach and traveling exhibit programming. By working in direct partnership with participating teachers, the project was tailored to the teachers' expressed desires and needs specific to their class needs and district requirements" (Eckhoff 263). Certainly, carefully considering the audience is important when designing Outreach programs.

Some outreach program staff serve as "ambassadors" for a museum in their community. The Ringling Museum of Art has a dedicated education staff—a coordinator and two teaching artists—focused entirely on outreach. They travel to communities around Sarasota, leading lessons and art-making with groups such as the Sarasota Housing Authority, the Boys and Girls Clubs of Manatee, and United Way Suncoast. As they state, "We hope these programs may be the spark that can change the trajectory of a life, impacting a family for generations to come" ("Teaching Artist Outreach Program").

Outreach, at times, may have nothing to do with art or a museum's collection, or even a responsive activity like those I describe. There are steps museums can take to build trust and relationships in a community that encourage visitors to eventually come through the doors of a museum. Museums can offer volunteers to local food pantries or food delivery services like Meals on Wheels. Museums can host once-a-year events like blood drives or food drives. Outreach may also come in the form of a pop-up exhibit around a community, or a museum may sponsor an artistic event like a free concert. Partnerships and outreach are crucial to diversifying museums' visitors and becoming a more integral part of a community's infrastructure.

Schools are also a key piece of the puzzle.

School Connections

Recently, I visited a small local museum with a narrow collection representing an Indigenous culture. The museum is tiny but beautiful, with an extensive collection presented in rotating exhibits. I talked with the museum's education manager who shared that they host very few K–12 school tours. Part of the reason is the size of the space, and entire grades normally have to be included on field trips. That made field trips within the district difficult. (There are often ways around this, however—this museum has a lovely outdoor space. Students can be broken out into smaller groups to participate in rotating indoor and outdoor activities—it just requires planning and volunteers.) The biggest obstacle, according to the education manager, is that the state educational standards do not include this particular region or cultural group in the curriculum at any grade level. Therefore, convincing schools to visit or take instructional time for a field trip or even class time for a traveling exhibit or program is a hard sell to administrators. As a result, despite having a one-of-a-kind rotating collection, a beautiful digitized gallery, an artist-in-residence, a museum educator, and a large group of volunteers, school tours to this museum are few and far between.

Schools look for obvious connections to educational standards, and sometimes, if they do not immediately recognized such standards, school systems and museums miss out on the opportunity to work together to enrich students' lives and experiences. For some museums, curricular connections are easily made to geography, social studies, science, or history standards. But for other museums—fine art museums for example—clear connections are challenging, particularly in the younger grades. Schools rely upon fine art curriculum standards; however, even standards related to the arts are challenging to make as arts education is squeezed out of many school system budgets. Looking for curricular connections in relation to particular thematic content and learning goals is not always easy.

For the purposes of this chapter, however, I want to consider other curricular connections and encourage museum educators to look for less obvious but equally important connections. Visitor Response Pedagogies offer opportunities for alternative curricular connections. In chapter 2, we discussed the importance of social-emotional learning (SEL) and transferable skills that are applicable to any content. We also reviewed how teachers at all levels are citing the need for support in the SEL of their students. However, if that is not enough of an argument to convince a school system to visit a museum or take advantage of museum programming, schools and museums can try to find other curricular connections related to SEL, wellness, or communication skills, just to name a few.

Let's use Florida state educational standards as our example.

The Florida standards of education provide an excellent example of how standards in different realms reinforce learning standards in a variety of ways. The obvious connection is through visual arts standards, and Florida outlines priorities for visual arts education in their statewide standards. Using these as a model, their "Big Ideas" ("Content Areas") articulate what students should know and what they should be able to do in grades K-12. The Big Ideas in visual arts for the state of Florida include (1) critical thinking and reflection, (2) historical and global connections, (3) innovations, technology, and the future, (4) organizational structure, and (5) skills, techniques, and processes. Although the Florida Standards of Education and their "Big Ideas" acknowledge the importance of guiding principles in visual and performing arts, the focus is more on connecting with people, fostering understanding, using art as a vehicle for expression, and refining transferable skills such as Critical Thinking. These guiding standards align well with a museum curriculum focused on Visitor Response Pedagogies. Museums have the opportunity to demonstrate these themes to students through experience and interaction with works in their collections. Looking specifically at the standards by grade level, these goals are apparent. For example, for grades one through five, Visual Arts Standard C-2 states that "assessing our own and others' artistic work, using critical thinking, problem-solving, and decision-making skills, is central to artistic growth" ("Visual Arts Standards"), clearly identifying important transferable skills in their application to artistic growth. These skills, however, play important roles in all academic and personal growth.

There are curricular connections in other academic areas as well. Looking at the Florida Standards in English Language Arts (ELA), for example, there are specific goals and benchmarks for reading and writing, organized by grade. For some activities, there may be easy connections (for example, the Group Poetry activity may meet some standards related to poetry or communication through writing). The most prevalent connection in ELA is in "Oral Communication" which is identified as a standard at every grade level, from kindergarten through twelfth grade. The expectations vary and build in a vertical or spiral progression. Using the sixth-grade standard as the median, it states that students will "present information orally, in a logical sequence, using nonverbal cues, appropriate volume, clear pronunciation, and appropriate pacing" ("ELA B.E.S.T. Standards"). For K–12, all students are expected to "use appropriate techniques and active listening skills when engaging in discussions in a variety of situations" ("ELA B.E.S.T. Standards"). These skills—Oral Communication, Active Listening, and Critical Thinking—are part of the seven transferable skills of Visitor Response Pedagogies, and VRP activities offer many opportunities for students at all grade levels to strengthen them.

Florida serves as one example, but there are similar applications with other state and local standards. For example, Loudoun County Public Schools in Virginia worked with the education team at Morven Park, the grounds and historic home of two governors, in reimagining their educational programming. Their student visitorship was low, mainly due to the fact that the historic figures and objects, as well as the time period, do not align with local and state curricula. The Morven Park education team shifted its focus to civic impact and education, using the site's history as a backdrop rather than a focus for its lessons. In 2014, they launched the Morven Park Center for Civic Impact (MPCCI) with a mission "to inspire a new generation of active and engaged community members by helping them develop their voice, research important issues, take responsibility, and make an impact" (Murtie et al. 158). Working with educators, they made connections to Loudoun County Public School standards focusing on skills such as communication, collaboration, critical thinking, creativity, and community contribution, among others.

Most educational standards recognize the important role transferable skills play in all aspects of learning. As a result, there are numerous paths to connecting VRP activities to state K–12 educational standards. The key is to move away from narrow content-focused standards (although those connections may be available as well) and think more broadly in terms of generalized skills that are reinforced through the experience or program.

Teacher Advisory Committees

To help make these connections and identify needs in the school system, teacher advisory committees are effective. For museums with a large education staff, these committees may not be necessary, particularly if the staff is large enough to have a designated school tour coordinator and a wide variety of expertise on staff. However, many museums have small education teams, sometimes composed of one or two educators. There are museums with no designated education staff that use volunteers to run tours and programs. Additionally, museum educators often do not have any background in teaching or education; instead, they are specialists in the field of art or science, with a passion for working with students and other visitors. In these cases, teacher advisory committees are invaluable.

Teacher advisory committees or teacher advisory boards are coalitions of educators from local school systems representing different grade levels working with museum staff to plan opportunities for local students. Before members are recruited, it is important to consider the role of the committee, structure expectations, and recruit members that share a passion for the museum and its offerings. I founded an educational advisory committee for a small local children's museum which had an education staff of one, an education manager. We developed it as a resource for the education manager and also as a way to get local schools more involved in the museum. We discussed ways to host more school groups, generated future plans for exhibits, and brainstormed community connections. For any teacher board or committee, educators offer realistic considerations for trips, themes, or topics that they prioritize, and they also identify needs in the community. An added benefit is that museums develop ongoing relationships with teachers and schools in the community. Chicago History Museum (CHM) educators Megan Clark and Heidi Moisan describe the process and advantages of creating such a board at CHM. One benefit is the identification of curricular connections, and these explorations are mutually beneficial for the museum staff and teachers. As one of their board members stated, "Many teachers think CHM is only for third grade because of the Illinois curriculum; since being on the Teacher Advisory Board, the teachers in my school from pre-K through eighth grade found new benefits for all grades" (Clark and Moisan 83).

Teachers are busy, so considering ways to seek and encourage true involvement on teacher boards is important. When I was chair of my local children's museum's educational advisory committee, it was hard to find the right time for meetings, for example, given the complexities and demands of teachers' schedules. The Chicago History Museum finds that perks help—offering museum memberships to educators, a free field trip bus, or free professional development training are some examples. Fundamentally, teachers want more ways to enrich their students' lives, and even if it means a few extra meetings, they will offer their time and expertise—and museums will gain invested educators, enthusiastic students, and many future museumgoers.

Virtual Learning

The digitization of museum collections began in earnest during the last decade, but the COVID-19 pandemic accelerated the pace of and demonstrated the need for virtual access to museum collections. While nothing replaces human contact and interaction, online collections are accessible and offer museums myriad ways to connect with their communities by using new, innovative digital or virtual learning programs. Simply put, online programming expands a museum's reach. Offering digital options is key with partnerships, outreach, and school connections. If people cannot stand in front of an artwork or object, having a high-quality image projected on a screen is pretty close to the real thing!

Moreover, multipart hybrid programs, with some experiences offered in person and some virtually, are also effective. As noted in "Museum Highlights" in chapter 3, the Ringling Museum of Art works with healthcare employees at Sarasota Memorial Hospital, offering a program that combines museum experiences, outreach experiences with a museum educator who travels to the hospital, and online sessions. With most museums digitizing their collections, options for virtual learning are numerous. For all of the activities listed in the VRP Activities Toolkit, utilizing digitized images is always an option and offers an entry point or gateway to the museum and hopefully, in time, an in-person visit.

Works Cited

"2022 Annual Performance Report." *Institute for Museum and Library Services*, Feb. 2023, https://www.imls.gov/publications/2022-annual-performance-report. Accessed 10 Aug. 2023.

Carlton, Lee. "Why Should Schools Practice Place-Based Learning?" *thinkglobalschool.org*, 5 July 2022. https://thinkglobalschool.org/why-should-schools-practice-place-based-learning/. Accessed 2 Aug. 2023.

Clark, Megan, and Heidi Moisan. "Creating an Effective Teacher Advisory Board." *Creating Meaningful Museum Experiences for K–12 Audiences*, edited by Tara Young, Rowman & Littlefield, 2021, pp. 83–90.

"Community Partnerships." *Studio Museum Harlem*, https://studiomuseum.org/community-partnerships. Accessed 5 Aug. 2023.

"Content Areas." *Florida Department of Education. CPALMS*, https://www.cpalms.org/Public/search/Standard. Accessed 10 August 2023.

Eckhoff, Angela. "Transformative Partnerships: Designing School-Based Visual Arts Outreach Programmes." *International Journal of Art and Design Education*, vol. 30, no. 2, June 2011, pp. 256–65. *Wiley Online*, https://doi.org/10.1111/j.1476-8070.2011.01701.x, Accessed 24 July 2023.

"ELA B.E.S.T. Standards." *Florida Department of Education*, https://www.fldoe.org/core/fileparse.php/7539/urlt/elabeststandardsfinal.pdf. Accessed 10 Aug. 2023.

Lung, Heidi. "Powerful Educational Partnerships: A State Museum Association Model for Access and Learning." *Creating Meaningful Museum Experiences for K–12 Audiences*, edited by Tara Young, Rowman & Littlefield, 2021, pp. 147–56.

Mac Murtie, Gwyneth, et al. "Into the Classroom: Making Museum Education Essential in School Curriculum." *Creating Meaningful Museum Experiences for K–12 Audiences*, edited by Tara Young, Rowman & Littlefield, 2021, pp. 157–65.

"Museums as Community Infrastructure." *Trendswatch*, American Alliance of Museums, 2022. https://www.aam-us.org/programs/center-for-the-future-of-museums/trendswatch-museums-as-community-infrastructure-2022/. Accessed 2 Aug. 2023.

"Teaching Artist Outreach Program." *Ringling Magazine*, The John and Mable Ringling Museum of Art, May–Sept. 2023, https://issuu.com/theringling/docs/issuu_r_mag_2023_may-sep/. Accessed 8 Aug. 2023.

"Visual Arts Standards." *Florida Department of Education. CPALMS*, https://www.cpalms.org/public/search/Standard. Accessed 10 Aug. 2022.

"What Is a Museum School and What Is It Like to Teach at One?" *We Are Teachers*, 13 May 2022, https://www.weareteachers.com/what-is-a-museum-school/. Accessed 12 Aug. 2022.

"Who We Are." *National Association of Museum Schools*, https://www.museumschools.org/history/. Accessed 10 Aug. 2023.

Chapter Six

The Questions We Ask

Implementing and Evaluating Visitor Response Pedagogies

So, you are ready to incorporate Visitor Response Pedagogies into your museum programming plan. Where do you start? Here are some considerations.

Defining Education

Although we discussed defining "education" earlier, it is worth circling back around to it. Particularly, if you are interested in implementing VRPs or other alternative programming, you need to have a shared understanding of its meaning and clearly defined goals related to its implementation. Most agree that education is at the heart of what museums do, but it is important to dig into what that means at your institution. This starts with the museum's mission and discussions with the staff, board, and volunteers.

There are important questions to ask and answer. Does education mean knowledge transfer? From where is that knowledge generated? Is it dependent on a curatorial narrative? How can the definition of education be expanded beyond knowledge transfer? What are ways educational programs can be more inclusive and impactful? In relation to VRPs and social-emotional learning, how can the museum's collection and exhibits help foster human connection, build community, and nurture transferable skills?

These are crucial discussions that result in a "pedagogical philosophy" that can "guide everything from program creation and staff training to interdivisional collaboration and community outreach . . . allow[ing] museums to go beyond mere fact transmission" (Hanley et al. 73). This pedagogical philosophy extends to divisions within education, including the definitions of partnering, outreach, and other realms of museum programming. I am a coordinator for youth and family programming at a large art museum, and this position required defining and ultimately reimagining the term "family." A family (for me and for my museum's programs) is not exclusive to a nuclear family or people who are even necessarily related. We cast a wide net with our use of the term "family" in relation to our programming, and we worked together to reach that definition.

Once these terms and understandings are articulated, it trickles down to other staff and volunteers, museum partners such as schools and organizations, and eventually to the visitors—the ones who count. But unless the ideological and definitional conversations occur, a museum runs the risk of "going down the rabbit hole of disconnected ideas" (Hanley 73).

Demographics

With the big, philosophical conversations completed, the next steps include understanding who your audience is and whom you want to see at your museum. This can, in broad strokes, be based on some basic visitor and observational data. Using an example from Chapter 5, Morven Park noticed they hosted very few school tours, and the ones they did host were mainly special occasion tours that took advantage of their spacious and beautiful grounds. They wanted to host more K–12 students, and they wanted the experiences to be more meaningful, so the Morven Park Center for Civic Impact was born.

Generalized data about museum populations points toward the need for more of . . . well, everything—more school connections, more partnerships, and more outreach. Diverse options hopefully lead to more visitors and community connections with more diverse populations. There is ample data that demonstrates Americans' esteem for museums; there are just distinct segments of the population that continue to struggle to find their place among them. The American Alliance of Museums' 2018 report on Museums and Public Opinion explored some key questions and found with their extensive survey that 97 percent of Americans believed that museums are educational for their community (Stein) but that attendance and access continue to be dominated by educated, white Americans, a trend that is not reflective of our increasing diversity. It is also not reflective of the belief that the museum of the future is one that is tightly connected to the community. Most research supports the need for greater reach and access, and that even single-visit museum experiences can make an impact for visitors. The National Art Education Association and the Association of Art Museum Directors sponsored a rigorous multisite research study in 2015 to look at the benefits of museum visits for students, concluding that emotional intelligence, awareness, self-value, and the role of creativity in life were by far the greatest outcomes of museum visits ("Survey of Single-Visit").

Large-scale studies and demographic data are useful, but collecting and analyzing local data about the makeup of visitors to your particular institution is equally important. Many museums collect detailed demographic information on their visitors, and museum educators can learn a lot from this by looking at breakdowns related to zip code, school districts, gender, race, and grade/age. This kind of information helps inform planning but also helps identify gaps in reach.

Mark Walhimer, in *Designing Museum Experiences*, advocates for identifying the "persona" of the visitor, or representative user (35). He writes that "empathy, which is the ability to put yourself in someone else's shoes, plays an important part in enhancing the museum visitor experience" (18). Using area demographics along with museum demographics allows staff to identify categories of visitors outside of those more traditional parameters. Grouping visitors by race or age leads to oversimplification of demographic data—for example, there are many geographical and cultural subcategories within the Hispanic community. Using other markers of a persona such as income level, interests, motivations, and education level helps connect more deeply with visitors' mindsets, thereby informing programming. Walhimer advocates for the use of "empathy maps" for different population segments, considering what, for example, a twenty-something local visitor may think, say, or feel (17). This may require some interviewing and research, but creating visitor personas allows museum staff to consider, for example, "How might this program impact a twenty-five-year-old male with no college degree who grew up locally as part of a Cuban American family?" Creating categories outside of traditional data points helps educators consider programming choices more deeply. John Falk, the founder of the Institute of Learning Innovation, developed visitor categories in his work *Identity and the Museum Visitor Experience*. These included Explorers (curiosity-driven), Facilitators (socially driven), Professionals/Hobbyists (those who feel a tie between the museum content and their profession/hobby), Experience Seekers (those who believe the museum is an important destination), and Rechargers (those seeking to have a contemplative, spiritual, or restorative experience) (Falk). Museum visitors may even occupy different personas on different days.

Generalized demographic data is vital in expanding a museum's reach through programming, but looking more closely at community needs and creating "personas" of visitors helps identify needs and design programs that prioritize specific goals.

Volunteers

To effectively facilitate programming, especially at museums with limited education staff, it is crucial to cultivate a robust team of museum volunteers. This is a key consideration that cannot be overlooked. There are many resources available for building a volunteer program, including the American Alliance of Museums toolkit "Designing a Museum Volunteer Program," which was released in 2019. This AAM toolkit is comprehensive, reviewing position descriptions, creating policies and training, and addressing evaluation and professional development. Perhaps the greatest consideration, and one that is receiving a great deal of attention, is recruiting diverse volunteers that accurately reflect our changing demographics.

Many museums are working to recruit a wide range of volunteers, which mainly continues to be mostly "an army of privileged old white women" (Haigney). This might be a bit of an exaggeration, but generally, docents and other museum volunteers have the bandwidth and availability to volunteer during weekdays, and they tend to be affluent, educated, and often retired individuals who spend a lot of time visiting museums. In order to make their museums more welcoming to visitors, some institutions prefer to use the term "guide" instead of "docent," viewing the former as a more approachable label. In 2021, the Art Institute of Chicago overhauled its sixty-year-old docent program as a step toward forging a stronger relationship with the highly diverse city that it serves. The board decided to "let go" of eighty-two docents and created a paid program of educators, stating that this change "allows community members of all income levels to participate, responds to issues of class and income inequity, and does not require financial flexibility to participate" (Pogrebin). Despite their intentions to reimagine more equitable educational staffing (which will eventually include the opportunity to apply for unpaid volunteer work), the Art Institute of Chicago received backlash for its decision.

This is not the only museum actively seeking diverse representation in all realms of museums, particularly with docents and educators who often have the most face time with museum visitors. Many museums are considering additional ways to diversify their volunteer positions. For example, the Getty Museum in Los Angeles attracts students into the volunteer pool by offering course credits. Other museums that rely on docents to deliver programming and cannot afford to lose them have turned their focus to training volunteers more rigorously. Many guide programs include training on race and implicit bias awareness. The Museum of Fine Arts in Boston is among those institutions rethinking their volunteer requirements, curriculum, and training rigor, bringing in outside consultants to educate volunteers on issues related to race and current events.

Instead of imposing a preconceived agenda or prepackaged educational goals, engaging in responsive activities encourages individual introspection and varied viewpoints. However, even these types of activities require shared language and responses to scenarios that volunteers may encounter. Training volunteers is key. And in the best case, museums can limit volunteers to those that are highly qualified and trained, representing a diverse demographic. This is either achieved by offering incentives such as memberships, museum perks, educational or professional credit—or in the best case, a wage.

Evaluation

Evaluation of educational programs informs important components such as staff, audience, interests, planning considerations, potential barriers to implementation, and impact. Writer and education professor George Hein explored how as museums evolved and became increasingly professionalized, the significance of museum evaluation became evident, prompting "important documentation of what a program is and examination to see if it meets its objectives . . . the increased pressures for accountability in museums—both from external economic factors and internal forces leading to increased professionalization—result in greater need for evaluation activities" (Hein 307). Hein also recognizes that all forms of evaluation can be helpful. Generally, museum educators should think about evaluation at all stages of programming: front end, formative, and summative.

Front-End Evaluation

Front-end evaluation is sometimes called "discovery" when museum professionals conduct research on a concept or idea they may have. Front-end evaluation includes research that explores a topic or strategy but also turns to the museum visitor to answer some of these questions. For example, museum staff can explore how much is known about a particular topic or strategy. Is there interest in the topic? What questions do visitors have about a specific topic? How likely would a visitor be to engage in a particular program or activity? In the best case, front-end evaluation may occur in tandem with exploration and evaluation related to an exhibit plan, with programming questions included in front-end exploratory work. This is why I think having an educator on an exhibit team is very valuable.

Front-end evaluation can take many forms. Methods may include in-person interviews, persona creation, empathy mapping, or online surveys. Thinking about key constituencies and the audience is important when asking people to complete whatever evaluative tool is developed. Offering an incentive for response may encourage participation and be worth the investment, such as a five-dollar voucher for the café or a similar discount off the price of admission. It could help save money in the long term by designing an exhibit, and specifically for this discussion an educational program, that resonates with visitors.

Formative Evaluation

Formative evaluation includes the process of collecting and analyzing feedback during the early phases of program development, planning, and initial implementation. It mainly occurs before the actual launch of a program. This may include prototyping or practice runs with staff or volunteers.

It may include sharing the program plan with other professionals and asking some key questions about content and presentation. It may include workshopping the program from the perspectives of various visitor "personas." The goal of formative evaluation is to anticipate issues or scenarios that might be encountered and have a plan in place to address them. For example, educators may prepare alternative explanations for activities or content. Educators may consider if there are adjustments or accommodations available for English language learners. These types of anticipatory considerations occur during this phase of evaluation.

Summative Evaluation

Some evaluation experts include an additional layer of evaluation, sometimes called remedial evaluation. This occurs after a program is launched and some initial evaluation occurs—it may be observational data such as "additional pencils are needed" or "cushions or stools may be helpful for people who find it hard to stand for the duration of a program." It may be related to the content or the actual activity, such as the need for smaller groups or written directions for visitors. As a classroom teacher, I constantly tweaked my plans and implementation of lessons. Most lesson plans are filled with notes reading, "Next time it would be helpful to. . ." or even "This did not work! Think of something new!"

Summative evaluation generally occurs at the end of a learning period or program. It looks at the goals of the program and assesses whether or not the goals were met. This can occur in several ways, using both quantitative and qualitative data. Quantitative data looks at things that can be measured with numbers—number of participants, breakdown of demographics of participants, average time the program took, costs, etc. Qualitative data is more conceptual. Did people enjoy the program? Was it worthwhile? What kind of change occurred—cognitively, emotionally—as a result of the program? Usually, this kind of data is collected through questionnaires, interviews, surveys, or Likert scales, and like most research, it is most reliable with a large, diverse sample size. Making sure that the evaluative tool is fair and approachable is crucial not only in achieving unbiased feedback but also in ensuring that the entirety of the program, including evaluation, feels safe and accessible for all participants.

The final steps in evaluation include bringing all of these phases together and interpreting the data. Sometimes this may require "converting" some of the qualitative data collected through interviews, surveys, and other means into quantitative data by coding and counting the most common responses. Then it is important to report, in some way, the major findings and overall perceptions of participants, using quotations or descriptive passages to illustrate particular findings.

Evaluation of museum programming is an important part of the visitor experience. A team of Korean researchers have proposed the use of "visitor-based social contextual information" (VSCI) to evaluate the visitor experience. VSCI is essentially the social information a visitor provides—feedback, reactions, and behavior. They collected VSCI by asking visitors to fill out evaluations, watching their behavior (using observation, tracking, timing, etc.), observing visitors' emotional responses to particular pieces and during programs, and by recording visitor comments (Yi et al. 25). This type of multipronged approach leads to robust and comprehensive data.

The Collaboration for Ongoing Visitor Experience Studies (COVES) is a project that includes over thirty museums and examines the questions we ask when collecting evaluative data. COVES asserts that "the questions we ask matter," as does the language we use in our questions. For example, it recommends removing the term "Superior" from evaluative surveys—a term which implies hierarchies sometimes associated with race—and instead using the term "Outstanding." These kinds of simple changes make a difference. One of the participating COVES museums, the Denver Museum of Nature and Science, wanted to ensure that the museum was using gender-inclusive language and asking questions in a sensitive way. The conversation ultimately led them to question why gender was relevant at all, and they eliminated questions related to gender from their demographic information. Institutions should decide what information is useful for them, but deeply considering questions and how they are asked is an important part of evaluation.

Evaluation should be built into educational programs, and as data is collected, it informs the creation of better education programs in the future. It also identifies gaps and weaknesses and allows us to correct those, resulting in improved visitor experiences and growth.

Works Cited

Falk, John H. *Identity and the Museum Visitor Experience*. Routledge, 2009.

Gold, Alexandra Ebert. *Museum Demographics Data Shows Inequity across All Fronts*. Medium .com, 5 May 2021, https://alexandraegold.medium.com/museum-demographics-data-shows -inequity-across-all-fronts. Accessed 14 Aug. 2023.

Haigney, Sophie. "Museums Have a Docent Problem." *Slate*, 18 Aug. 2020. https://slate.com/ culture/2020/08/museums-train-white-docents-talk-race-art.html. Accessed 15 Aug. 2023.

Hanley, Jason, et al. "A Pedagogical Philosophy as a Guiding Light for Museum Education Depart-ments." *Creating Meaningful Museum Experiences for K–12 Audiences*, edited by Tara Young, Rowman & Littlefield, 2021, pp. 73–81.

Hein, George. "Evaluation of Museum Programmes and Exhibits." *The Educational Role of the Museum*, edited by Eilean Hooper-Greenhill, Routledge, 1999, pp. 306–12, *ResearchGate*, file:/// Users/ameswinter/Desktop/Visitor%20Response%20 Pedagogies/Evaluation_of_museum _programmes_and_exhibits.pdf. Accessed 16 Aug. 2023.

"Museums and Public Opinion." *American Alliance of Museums*, Jan. 2018, https://www.aam-us .org/wp-content/uploads/2018/04/Museums-Public-Opinion-FINAL.pdf. Accessed 14 Aug. 2023.

Pogrebin, Robin. "Art Institute of Chicago Ends a Docent Program, and Sets Off a Backlash." *New York Times*, 21 Oct. 2021, https://www.nytimes.com/2021/10/21/arts/design/chicago-art -institute-docents.html. Accessed 15 Aug. 2023.

"Survey of Single-Visit K–12 Art Museum Programs." *National Art Education Association and Asso-ciation of Art Museum Directors*, Randi Korn and Associates, 2015, https://arteducators-prod .s3.amazonaws.com/documents/. Accessed 14 Aug. 2023.

Walhimer, Mark. *Designing Museum Experiences*. Rowman & Littlefield, 2022.

Yi, Taeha, et al. "The Influence of Visitor-Based Social Contextual Information on Visitors' Museum Experience." *PLOS One*, vol. 17, no. 5, 24 May 2022, https://journals.plos.org/ plosone/article?id=10.1371/journal.pone.0266856. Accessed 16 Aug. 2023.

Appendix A

What happened before?

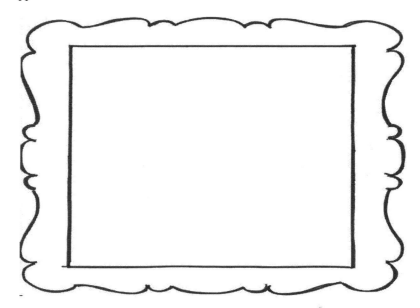

What happened after?

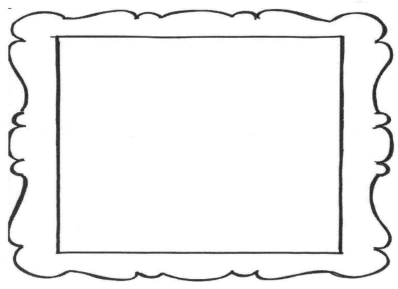

Before and After. *Source:* Author.

Appendix B

My Basic Emotions

These emotions will be combined to create complex emotions

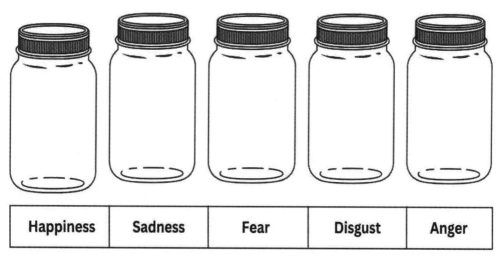

Happiness	Sadness	Fear	Disgust	Anger

Color your emotions. *Source:* Author.

Complex Emotions

Color your emotions. *Source:* Author.

Appendix C

Curator Challenge. *Source:* Author.

Appendix D

---

5 things you can see. . . . .

4 things you can/could touch. . . .

3 things can can/could hear. . . .

2 things you can/could smell. . . .

1 thing you can/could taste. . . .

---

5 things you can see. . . . .

4 things you can/could touch. . . .

3 things can can/could hear. . . .

2 things you can/could smell. . . .

1 thing you can/could taste. . . .

---

5 4 3 2 1 Grounding Technique Cards. *Source:* Author.

Appendix E

Thought bubbles for imagined conversations. *Source:* Author.

Appendix F

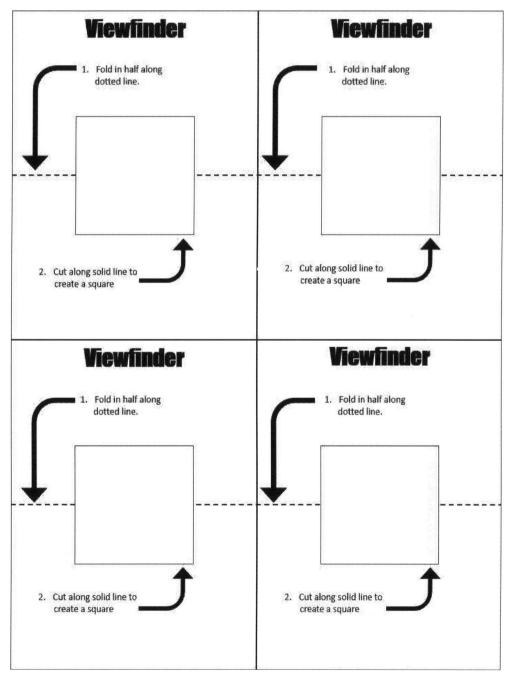

Viewfinder template. *Source:* Author.

Index

About the Author

Ames Morton-Winter, MA Ed, ALM, received her bachelor of arts in history from the University of Virginia, a master's degree in education—curriculum and teaching from the College of William and Mary, and a master's degree in liberal arts—museum studies from Harvard University. She has spent more than two decades teaching history, English, and English as a second language in public schools. She has worked with museums in many capacities, including as a volunteer, an educational consultant, a board member/chair, and a museum educator. Currently, she is the coordinator for youth and family programming at The John and Mable Ringling Museum of Art in Sarasota, Florida. She collaborates with a team of nine educators on a sprawling museum campus spanning sixty-six acres, comprising diverse venues and collections. Her background in education and curriculum development, passion for museum collections, and belief in inclusive teaching practices culminated in *Purposeful Museum Programming Using Visitor Response Pedagogies.*

Purposeful Museum Programming Using Visitor Response Pedagogies